THE STRUGGLE
FOR IDENTIY
ISLAM AND THE WEST

Tayyib Omar

MASON CREST
PHILADELPHIA

Mason Crest
450 Parkway Drive, Suite D
Broomall, PA 19008
www.masoncrest.com

©2017 by Mason Crest, an imprint of National Highlights, Inc.

Printed and bound in the United States of America.

CPSIA Compliance Information: Batch #UI2016.
For further information, contact Mason Crest at 1-866-MCP-Book.

First printing
1 3 5 7 9 8 6 4 2

Library of Congress Cataloging-in-Publication Data

on file at the Library of Congress
ISBN: 978-1-4222-3678-9 (hc)
ISBN: 978-1-4222-8116-1 (ebook)

Understanding Islam series ISBN: 978-1-4222-3670-3

Table of Contents

KEY ICONS TO LOOK FOR:

Words to Understand: These words with their easy-to-understand definitions will increase the reader's understanding of the text, while building vocabulary skills.

Sidebars: This boxed material within the main text allows readers to build knowledge, gain insights, explore possibilities, and broaden their perspectives by weaving together additional information to provide realistic and holistic perspectives.

Research Projects: Readers are pointed toward areas of further inquiry connected to each chapter. Suggestions are provided for projects that encourage deeper research and analysis.

Text-Dependent Questions: These questions send the reader back to the text for more careful attention to the evidence presented there.

Series Glossary of Key Terms: This back-of-the book glossary contains terminology used throughout this series. Words found here increase the reader's ability to read and comprehend higher-level books and articles in this field.

Introduction

by Camille Pecastaing, Ph.D.

Islam needs no introduction. Everyone around the world old enough is likely to have a formed opinion of Islam and Muslims. The cause of this wide recognition is, sadly, the recurrent eruptions of violence that have marred the recent—and not so recent—history of the Muslim world. A violence that has also selectively followed Muslim immigrants to foreign lands, and placed Islam at the front and center of global issues.

Notoriety is why Islam needs no simple introduction, but far more than that. Islam needs a correction, an exposition, a full discussion of its origins, its principles, its history, and of course of what it means to the 1.5 to 2 billion contemporaries associated with it, whether by origins, tradition, practice or belief.

The challenge is that Islam has a long history, spread over fourteen centuries. Its principles have been contested from the beginning, the religion has known schism after schism, and politico-theological issues instructed all sorts of violent conflict. The history of Islam is epic, leaving Islam today as a mosaic of diverse sects and practices: Sunnism, Shi'ism, Sufism, Salafism, Wahhabism, and of course, Jihadism. The familiarity of those terms often masks ignorance of the distinctions between them.

Islam is many things to many people, and while violent radicals occupy the headlines, what a Muslim is in the 21st century is practically indefinable. Islam is present on every continent; the religion of billionaires and of the poorest people in the world, the religion of kings and revolutionaries, of illiterate pastoralists and nuclear scientists, of fundamentalist theologians and avant-garde artists. Arabic is the language of Islam, the language of the Qur'an, but most Muslims only speak other tongues. Many Muslims indulge in moderate consumption of alcohol without feeling that they have renounced their faith. Boiled down to its simplest expression, being Muslim in the 21st century is an appreciation for one's origins and a reluctance to eat pork.

It is not only non-Muslims who have a partial view of Islam. Muslims, too, have a point of view limited by their own experience. This tunnel vision is often blamed for the radicalization that takes place at the margins of Islam. It is because they do not fully apprehend the diversity and complexity of their faith that some follow the extremist views of preachers of doom and violence. Among those, many are converts, or secularized Muslims who knew and cared little about religion until they embraced radicalism. Conversely, the foundation of deradicalization programs is education: teaching former militants about the complexity of the Islamic tradition, in particular the respect for the law and tolerance of diversity that Prophet Muhammad showed when he was the ruler of Medinah.

Islam in the 21st century is a political religion. There are four Islamic republics, and other states that have made Islam their official religion, bringing Islamic law (Shari'a) in varying degrees into their legal systems. Wherever multiparty elections are held, from Morocco to Indonesia, there are parties representing political Islam. Some blame Islam's political claims for the relative decline of the Muslim world. Once a center of wealth and power and knowledge, it now lags behind its European and East Asian neighbors, still struggling to transition from a rural, agrarian way of life to the urban, now post-industrial age. But for others, only Islam will deliver a successful and indigenous modernization.

Islam is also an economic actor. Shari'a instructs the practices of what is known as Islamic finance, a sector of the international financial system that oversees two trillion dollars worth of assets. For decades now, Islamist organizations have palliated the deficiencies of regional states in the provision of social services, from education to healthcare, counseling, emergency relief, and assistance to find employment. It is the reach of Islamist grassroots networks that has insured the recent electoral success of Islamic parties. Where the Arab Spring brought liberalization and democratization, Islam was given more space in society, not less.

It should be clear to all by now that modernity, and post-modernity, is not absolute convergence toward a single model—call it the Western, secular, democratic model. Islam is not a legacy from a backward past that refuses to die, it is also a claim to shape the future in a new way. Post-communist China is making a similar claim, and there may be others to come, although today none is as forcefully and sometimes as brutally articulated as Islam's. That only would justify the urgency to learn about Islam, deconstruct simplistic stereotypes and educate oneself to the diversity of the world.

1

Islam and the West

In February 2016, US President Barack Obama visited the Islamic Society of Baltimore because of what his administration perceived as an increase in anti-**Muslim** attitudes in the United States. Violence and discrimination against Muslims in the West had increased in response to recent terrorist attacks by Muslims in Paris and in San Bernardino, California. The negative attitudes toward Muslims was fueled by candidates who were competing in the American presidential primaries.

Describing conversations with young Muslim parents whose children were worried that they would be removed from the country, Obama attempted to change what he felt were unfair beliefs about Muslims and terrorism, and said that people of all faiths should be accepted without bias into the United States.

"Let me say as clearly as I can as president of the United States: you fit right here," Obama told several thousand Muslims at the

"I know that in Muslim communities across our country, this is a time of concern and, frankly, a time of some fear," President Obama said in his 2016 speech at a Baltimore mosque. "Like all Americans, you're worried about the threat of terrorism. But on top of that, as Muslim Americans, you also have another concern—and that is your entire community so often is targeted or blamed for the violent acts of the very few."

Islamic Society of Baltimore. "You're right where you belong. You're part of America too. You're not Muslim or American. You're Muslim and American."

President Obama had previously visited mosques in other countries—most notably delivering a speech addressed to the Muslim world from Cairo, Egypt, in June 2009— but had not previously visited a mosque in the United States, the Associated Press reported. But Obama's mosque visit, and his remarks about Islam and its place in American life, had a noteworthy precedent. A few days after the September 11, 2001, terrorist attacks, in which Muslim terrorists crashed airplanes into the World Trade Center and the Pentagon, causing about 3,000 deaths, then-President George W. Bush had visited the Islamic Center in Washington, D.C.

Bush declared that the United States would fight against terrorism, but tried to clearly explain that the United States was not at war with Muslims, but only with people willing to use terror as a political tool. In the wake of the September 11 attacks, it was obvious that many ***devout*** Muslims, both US citizens and people who live in other parts of the world, were just as shocked and saddened by the attacks as non-Muslims. "The face of terror is not the true faith of Islam," Bush had said. "That's not what Islam is all about. Islam is peace."

In the aftermath of the September 11 attacks, some people asked how it was possible for one religion to be the source of such remarkably different attitudes and actions. Others wondered why Muslims would use terror to try to achieve their aims, why there is anger against the United States and other Western nations throughout the Islamic world, and whether there could ever be peace between Muslims and non-Muslims.

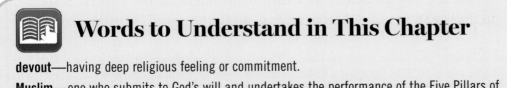

Words to Understand in This Chapter

devout—having deep religious feeling or commitment.

Muslim—one who submits to God's will and undertakes the performance of the Five Pillars of Islamic faith.

The people who ask these questions often know very little about Islam, the history of the relationships between Muslim and Western countries, or the current relationships between the United States and the Muslim world. They may not realize that Islam is the fastest-growing religion in the world. There are nearly 2 billion Muslims—about 24 percent of the global population—making Islam the world's second-largest religion. And Muslims are not strange people living in faraway lands—there are thriving Muslim communities throughout North America. Today, it is estimated that between three million and eight million Muslims live in the United States, making Islam the third-largest religion in the country. Another million Muslims live in Canada.

For more than 1,400 years, the Muslim and Western worlds have interacted. Some of today's areas of conflict are rooted in events that took place hundreds of years ago. An understanding of the past will help people of all faiths and nationalities to better understand current events, and make it possible for people to live and work together, to respect and appreciate each other, and to thrive together as members of a multicultural global society.

Text-Dependent Questions

1. What mosque did Barack Obama visit in February 2016?
2. About how many Muslims live in the United States? How many live in Canada?

Research Project

There are many different definitions of what terrorism is. Each person in your class should research recent news items to find examples of terrorist acts. Discuss these examples. Keeping in mind the contexts of the attacks, as well as the ideologies of the groups that committed them, what are the common elements, and how is each one different? Ask members of the group to try to define terrorism, and discuss the pros and cons of each definition. Consider the following questions: What differentiates terrorists from warriors, freedom fighters, or patriots? Is any attack on civilians a terrorist act? When governments bomb cities, is it terrorism?

2

The Birth of Islam

In Mecca, an ancient city in present-day Saudi Arabia, there stands an old square building known as the Kaaba. According to Islamic tradition, Adam, the first man, originally built the Kaaba as a place of worship. It is said that after the first building was destroyed, a second building was erected by Abraham, a man who is considered a patriarch by three major world religions—Judaism, Christianity, and Islam. Abraham, the Muslims believe, was helped by his son Ishmael, from whom the Arabs are said to be descended. The ancient Kaaba, which still stands today, has been renovated several times over the centuries. A sacred black stone (probably a meteorite) is located in one wall of the structure. Muslims consider the Kaaba the holiest site in the world.

Some 14 centuries ago, a season of severe storms damaged the building. The leaders of the four major tribes of Mecca agreed that the expense of repairing the Kaaba would be shared equally among all the

Opposite: American Muslims prostrate themselves during Friday prayers outside their mosque in Queens, New York. Islam is one of the world's major religions, and there are an estimated 6.5 million Muslims living in the United States and Canada.

tribes. However, when the project was almost complete, a dispute arose. The leaders could not agree which tribe should have the honor of replacing the sacred black stone. According to tradition, a man named Muhammad devised a solution that pleased everyone. He placed the black stone in the center of a large cloth. The leader of each tribe held one corner of the cloth, lifted the stone, and carried it into the Kaaba, where Muhammad slid the stone off the cloth and into place. This solution settled the argument fairly by allowing all of the tribes to share the honor of replacing the stone.

Muhammad was much more than a man who could solve problems and help people work together. During his lifetime he spread the message that there is no god but *Allah*. The religion known as Islam developed from Muhammad's teachings; Muslims believe these teachings came directly from Allah, and revere Muhammad as Allah's last, and most important, prophet.

The Life of Muhammad

Muhammad ibn Abdullah was born in Mecca in CE 570. Throughout his childhood he experienced much sorrow. Muhammad never knew his father, who died just a few weeks before he was born. His mother died when he was just six years old. After his mother died Muhammad lived with his grandfather, who died when Muhammad was eight years old. After his grandfather died, Muhammad lived with his uncle. Because Muhammad had to help the family by taking care of sheep, he was not able to attend school. Consequently, he never learned to read and write.

Because he had experienced so much tragedy in his own childhood, as

---

 Words to Understand in This Chapter

Allah—"the God"; the one God that Muslims worship.

mosque—Muslim place of worship.

Ramadan—the month in which Muhammad received his first revelations; the traditional month of fasting for all Muslims.

The Great Mosque of Mecca is filled with Muslim worshippers making the annual pilgrimage to the holy city. The mosque contains the most sacred Islamic shrine, the Kaaba, a square black building believed to have originally been built by Adam.

an adult Muhammad was sensitive to the needs of orphans, widows, slaves, and other poor people. He taught that a community has a duty to help its neediest members. This teaching became one of the five pillars, or required duties, of Islam.

When Muhammad was 25 years old he married a rich businesswoman named Khadija. They met when Muhammad agreed to sell some of Khadija's goods in Syria. According to Khadija's servant, who traveled with Muhammad, two amazing things happened on the trip from Mecca to Damascus. The first incident occurred as Muhammad was resting under a tree. A Christian monk told the servant that the man sitting beneath the tree was a prophet. The second incident happened as the group traveled across the desert. One day when the sun was high overhead, the servant looked at Muhammad and saw two angels shielding him from the heat. When the group returned the servant reported these events to Khadija. Muhammad had already impressed her because he had sold her goods at a large profit. When Khadija heard her servant's report she became even more fascinated with Muhammad and asked him why he was not married. He answered that he was too poor to support a family. The wealthy Khadija proposed to Muhammad, and they soon married. Muhammad and Khadija had four daughters, as well as two sons who died in childhood.

As Muhammad grew older, he became widely respected as a wise and honest man. Every year Muhammad traveled to a cave called Ghar Hira, which was located a few miles outside of Mecca, to fast and pray during the month of *Ramadan*. When Muhammad was about 40 years old, as he meditated in the cave, he evaluated the Arab society around him. He saw a cruel culture that needed spiritual and social reform.

Mecca was a very wealthy center of international trade. This financial success created a climate in which people competed ferociously for money. In addition to being greedy, people were not taking care of the poor in their communities. Care for the disadvantaged had once been a tradition among Arab tribes, but Muhammad felt this value was disappearing from his society. Women in pre-Islamic Arabia were oppressed and brutally abused. They were denied the right to inherit property and had no rights if they were divorced. Pre-Islamic Meccans believed that girl children might bring shame to their families or were bad luck, so some parents killed their own young daughters.

Muhammad also disagreed with the polytheism followed by many Arabs. The people of Arabia were familiar with the monotheistic religions of the Jews and Christians who lived in the Middle East and Northern Africa. Some Arabs believed that one god, Allah, had created heaven and earth, and was supreme above all other gods. However, many of the people of Mecca also worshiped idols—statues made of stone or clay.

The Prophet Receives Allah's Message

As Muhammad meditated about these things in Ghar Hira, an angel appeared to him. Muhammad felt like he was being squeezed very tightly.

Then the angel began speaking to Muhammad, revealing the first of many messages later recorded in the Qur'an (the holy writings on which Islam is based). Muhammad was frightened and confused by this event. When he returned home he told only his wife and a cousin about what had happened to him. Khadija and her cousin comforted Muhammad and assured him that Allah had chosen him for a special purpose. In spite of their encouragement, Muhammad did not publicly preach the message given by the angel for two years. He did, however, speak privately with people about Allah's message, and soon developed a core of loyal followers.

According to the Qur'an, one night the Angel Gabriel took Muhammad from the Kaaba in Mecca to the city of Jerusalem, where the ancient Jewish temple had stood. Muhammad then ascended to heaven, where he met Allah and had an opportunity to speak with such revered

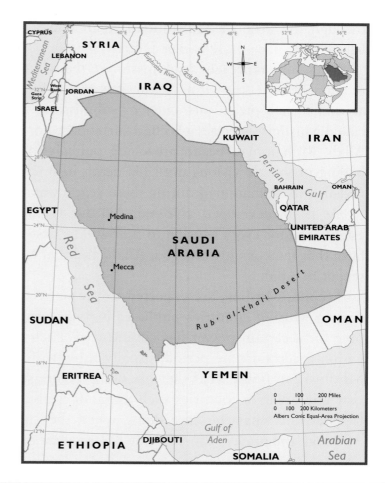

This map shows the present-day boundaries of Saudi Arabia, where the holy cities Mecca and Medina are located, as well as the borders of other countries on the Arabian Peninsula. Islam spread throughout the peninsula during the seventh century.

Jewish and Christian figures as Abraham, Moses, and Jesus. This is one of the reasons Jerusalem plays a central role in Islamic theology. Muslim scholars disagree on whether Muhammad was elevated physically to heaven, or only spiritually with his body remaining static. However, what is most important about this event, known as Muhammad's Night Journey, is that it affirmed Muhammad's belief that Allah required him to preach a return to the true monotheistic faith. After returning from his Night Journey, Muhammad asserted that he had been sent by Allah to remind Jews and Christians about the important precepts they had forgotten over the ages.

Although Muslims respect certain figures and traditions of the earlier Jewish and Christian religions—for example, all of these religions revere Abraham as an important patriarch—Muslims do not believe that Islam is an offshoot of either of these faiths. Instead, the Qur'an asserts that through the Prophet Muhammad Allah sent a new and final religion, Islam, to replace those earlier faiths.

Muhammad preached submission to the will of Allah, and so the new religion became known as Islam, a word derived from the Arabic verb *aslama*, which means surrender or submission. Followers of Islam were called Muslims—people who had surrendered or submitted to the will of Allah. Muhammad began preaching publicly in 612, and he continued having prophetic visions until his death in 632. The word of Allah, as revealed to Muhammad during these years, was recorded in the Qur'an.

As Islam developed, five required duties (the pillars of Islam) were established for every Muslim to follow. The first is a simple profession of faith that there is only one god, Allah, and that Muhammad was the messenger of Allah.

Second, Muslims are expected to pray at five designated times each day. In Muslim countries public calls to prayer remind people that the time for a certain prayer has commenced. Each prayer must be finished within a certain time period, usually three to four hours, so in general Muslims can finish what they are doing before starting their prayers. (In very conservative countries such as Saudi Arabia, Muslims are expected to interrupt what they are doing when they hear the call to prayer.) Although the prayers can be made in a *mosque* or place of worship, most

Muslims pray at home or in another clean environment. Muslims are expected to face the direction of Mecca when they pray. On Fridays, Muslims go to the mosque for community prayers.

The third pillar is a tradition of giving to the poor. Muslims pay an annual tax—traditionally, 2.5 percent of one's total wealth—and this money is supposed to be distributed to those in need. In many Muslim societies, older people or disabled people rely on income from this tax, almost like the social security program in the United States.

Fourth, Muslims fast during Ramadan, the ninth month of the Islamic calendar. During the fast Muslims eat a meal before sunrise, fast through-

Muslims believe that Allah is the same God that followers of the other major monotheistic faiths, Judaism and Christianity, follow. Because of this, Muslims share some historical traditions with Jews and Christians, and Jerusalem is considered the second-holiest city in Islam, after Mecca but before Medina. (Above) Jesus meets his mother, Mary, on the way to his crucifixion. This carving appears on a building along the Via Dolorosa, the route through Jerusalem that Jesus is believed to have followed while carrying the cross. (Left) An Orthodox Jew prays while facing the Western Wall, the only remaining part of the ancient Jewish temple in Jerusalem.

out the daylight hours, and eat an evening meal after sunset. Muslims are also expected to abstain from tobacco use and certain other physical activities during this time period. The month of fasting ends with a special celebration called the Feast of Breaking the Fast (Eid al-Fitr). This typically is a joyful occasion for eating special meals and giving gifts.

Fifth, Muslims must make at least one pilgrimage to Mecca during their lifetime, if they are physically and financially able to do so. The annual pilgrimage season starts shortly after Ramadan. Today, approximately two million Muslims make the journey to Mecca every year. When they arrive in Mecca they participate in a series of special ceremonies over a period of five days. Out of piety, some Muslims make the pilgrimage several times during a lifetime.

Persecution of the Early Muslims

Most of Muhammad's early followers were poor people and women. Muhammad's message appealed to them because he wanted to establish a community that would treat all of its members fairly and respectfully. However, some people—particularly the rich and powerful leaders of Meccan society—opposed Muhammad. These wealthy and influential critics felt that Muhammad's message of monotheism and social justice threatened their livelihoods. For one thing, pilgrims came from all over Arabia to worship idols that were kept in the Kaaba. These pilgrims were a source of income for local merchants. If people worshiped only Allah, they would no longer need to travel to Mecca to worship these gods. Additionally, Muhammad preached that the rich should share their wealth with the poor—an idea that was not particularly popular among the rich.

The leaders of Mecca believed that Muhammad wanted to take control of the city. Muhammad insisted that he was only a messenger from Allah, not a ruler, but the leaders did not believe this claim and harassed Muhammad and his followers. They passed laws prohibiting all business and social relations between Muslims and non-Muslims. The Meccans also reneged on contracts and deals with Muslims and usurped many Muslim homes and properties. As a result, Muslims living in Mecca could not earn a living. Some even starved to death.

At the same time, the Meccans targeted and tortured Muslims, especially those who were poor and powerless. A man named Abu Yasir and his wife, Umm Yasir, were killed because of their faith, becoming the first martyrs of Islam. They would not be the last. Among the Muslims who died during this time of suffering was Muhammad's wife Khadija. The Meccan leaders also plotted to kill Muhammad and his prominent followers, but the plot failed. Ultimately, this oppression forced the Muslims to begin looking for a new home outside of Mecca.

In 620 representatives from Yathrib, a city in Arabia approximately 250 miles north of Mecca, asked Muhammad to come to their city and settle their disputes. The tribes of the region had been engaged in violent warfare for many years. They were slaughtering each other and urgently needed someone to help them make peace. In 622, after the plot to assassinate Muhammad was uncovered, Muhammad and the Muslims left Mecca and moved to Yathrib. This important event is known as the *hijra*, from an Arabic word meaning to migrate or to leave one's tribe.

In the Arab world of the seventh century, the act of leaving Mecca was a difficult social adjustment. The tribe was the basis of Arab society. Members of a tribe were bound together by blood relationships and by moral and social obligations. When Muhammad and his followers left Mecca, they assumed all responsibilities for their own defense, but in the eyes of their Meccan relatives they also abandoned their responsibilities to defend other members of their tribe. The relatives they left behind in Mecca vowed to destroy the Muslims who had rejected their families and traditions.

Growth of the Muslim Community

When Muhammad arrived in Yathrib, he helped the tribal leaders resolve their differences. Then he established the first Muslim community. The first mosque was built next to Muhammad's house, and it became the center of religious and social activity for the Muslims. Even though Muhammad did not force any of the city's inhabitants to convert to Islam, many chose to become Muslims. Islamic ideas soon became the basis of the

The Prophet's Mosque in Medina is considered one of the most sacred sites in Islam. While Muhammad lived in Medina, he and his followers established the first Muslim government. The Muslims eventually grew strong enough to force Mecca to submit, and spread their religion throughout the Arabian Peninsula.

city's judicial and social systems and the name of the city was changed to Medina, "the prophet's city."

In Islamic thought the *umma*, the Muslim community, is the basis of all social relations. Membership in the *umma* is more binding than membership in a family or tribe. Members of the *umma* must protect and defend each other regardless of their previous tribal relations. This pact of mutual defense applied to the entire community—Muslim and non-Muslim. If any group within the *umma* was threatened, the rest of the *umma* was obliged to defend them. The concept of *umma* supplanted the traditional Arab notion of obligations based on blood relationships. Acceptance of this new social ideal was an important act of faith for the Muslims and for the non-Muslims who lived among them in Medina.

Muhammad established alliances with non-Muslim Arab tribes by contracting politically beneficial marriages. Multiple marriages were common in this era, and the regular wars between tribes meant that women often lost their husbands. Widowhood left these women without male protectors in a society that traditionally treated women harshly. Muhammad's marriages allowed him to protect some of these widows and make their lives more comfortable than they would have been otherwise.

The cities of Medina and Mecca were at war with each other from 624 to 628, when a peace treaty was negotiated. In 629 the Meccans broke the treaty and the war resumed. The fighting ended in 630 when Muhammad led an army of 10,000 Muslims and their allies to Mecca. Disheartened, outnumbered, and surrounded, the Meccans surrendered without a fight. After the conquest of Mecca, many people living in the city decided to become Muslims.

During the next few years, Muhammad and his followers spread Islam throughout the Arabian Peninsula. Within a few years after Muhammad's death in 632, most Arabs were Muslims and the people of the peninsula were united politically and religiously for the first time in history.

Text-Dependent Questions

1. In what month did Muhammad receive his original revelations from Allah?
2. Who opposed Muhammad when he began preaching in Mecca? Why?
3. In what city did Muhammad establish the first Muslim community?

Research Project

Using your school library or the Internet, do some research to find out about what Muslims think of the holy figures of the Judeo-Christian tradition, such as Abraham, Moses, and Jesus Christ. What do Muslims believe about these Biblical figures? How does that differ from what Jews and Christians think of them? Write a one-page paper listing the differences between the various religious traditions.

3

The Expansion of Islam

Muhammad's death marked a critical moment for Islam. The early Muslims had to deal with several major issues. Perhaps the most important question was who would follow Muhammad as leader of the *umma*, because the prophet had died without clearly choosing a successor.

Some Muslims did not want to choose a single Islamic leader to follow Muhammad. They suggested that each tribe should elect its own imam, or religious leader. However, other Muslims opposed this idea, because they were concerned that multiple religious leaders would ultimately undermine the unity of the Muslims. These people proposed that the umma should elect one leader to guide all of the Muslims. Eventually it was decided that the *umma* would select a single leader, or *caliph* (from the Arabic word for deputy or successor). The caliph would serve as the political, military, and religious leader of the Muslims.

Opposite: This page from a twelfth-century Arabic manuscript shows a caravan passing a fortified town. Trading was an important part of life in the desert, and helped disseminate ideas, cultural beliefs, and technology throughout the Arabian Peninsula. Arab traders helped spread Islam into Africa and Asia.

Next, the Muslims had to decide how the caliph would be chosen. Some people thought the succession should be hereditary, because they believed a leader transmitted special qualities to his heirs or descendants. Muhammad's closest surviving male relative was his son-in-law, Ali ibn Ali Talib, and some Muslims believed that Ali had inherited Muhammad's leadership qualities. Others believed that the leader of the *umma* should be chosen because of his ability, wisdom, and the strength of his faith, rather than on a hereditary basis.

A man named Abu Bakr was chosen as the first caliph in 632. He had been a close friend of Muhammad, one of the earliest converts to Islam, and the father of the prophet's second wife Aisha. Abu Bakr was not a blood relative of Muhammad, which indicated that the caliphs would not be selected on the basis of heredity. Ali's supporters, who wanted the leadership to be hereditary, disagreed with the election process and its results. This disagreement would eventually lead to the most important schism in the history of Islam, the division of the faith into Sunni and Shia branches.

Although Muhammad had proclaimed the fundamentals of the Islamic faith, the early caliphs and the societies they ruled continued to develop and debate the faith for centuries. This evolving nature of the Islamic faith guaranteed the viability and adaptability of Islam through the centuries.

After the leadership issue was resolved, another important problem had to be faced. Some Arab tribes that had converted to Islam and signed treaties with Muhammad believed their obligations had ended when he died. Some renounced the faith. Others refused to pay taxes to a central government, arguing that the zakat should be paid to local leaders. These rebellions are known in Islamic history as the Apostasy Wars, but they were quickly suppressed under the leadership of the first caliph. By the time Abu Bakr died in

Words to Understand in This Chapter

caliph—"successor" or "deputy"; political leader of Sunni Muslims.
dhimmi—a non-Muslim protected by Muslim rulers; this status required payment of a special tax.

634, the Arabs were more strongly united than they had been before, and the Islamic kingdom was twice as large as it had been under Muhammad's leadership.

During the ten-year reign of the second caliph, Umar al-Khattab, the Islamic faith began to spread throughout the Middle East. Muslim armies conquered Egypt and Syria, which had belonged to the Byzantine empire. The Muslims also conquered the area of modern-day Iraq, which had been part of the Persian empire.

The Byzantine empire was the eastern half of the ancient Roman empire. From its center in the city of Constantinople (in modern-day Turkey), it had survived the fall of the Roman empire in the fifth century. Until the rise of Islam the Byzantines

This page from a book about Ali is illustrated with scenes from his life. Ali was one of Muhammad's closest companions, and some people felt that the Prophet had chosen him to become his heir and leader of the Muslims. However, after Muhammad's death another of the Prophet's companions, Abu Bakr, was selected as the first caliph.

ruled over a large part of the Middle East and North Africa. Persia, to the east of the Arabian Peninsula (the area of modern-day Iran), had been the home of many powerful empires throughout the ages. In the early seventh century the land was ruled by the Sassanid dynasty of kings.

The emergence of Islam marked the start of a period of decline for both of these empires. There were several reasons for this. In the centuries that preceded Islam, Byzantine and Persian forces had fought frequent wars, which exhausted the energies and resources of both empires. Also, the imperial governments of both the Byzantines and Persians had become very repressive, particularly of people living in territories on the fringes of their empires. As the relationship between the imperial governments and the territories that they controlled became more exploitative, the rulers no longer enjoyed the allegiance of the people living in these territories. This played an important role in the effectiveness of the Islamic forces in gaining the allegiance of these territories after Muslim armies defeated the imperial forces.

The Arab conquests of the seventh century were motivated in part by the fact that the Middle East is a difficult place to live. Conquest of wealthier neighbors was one way of ensuring Arab survival. Additionally, the newly united Arabs may have experienced a pride and confidence that they had never felt before. Arab strength, combined with Byzantine and Persian weakness, enabled the Arabs to conquer much of the region very quickly.

Most important, perhaps, was the desire of the Muslims to spread their religion throughout the world. As the Arab armies succeeded, they offered the people they conquered a chance to convert to Islam. This was supposed to be a free decision. The Qur'an explicitly forbids the forcible conversion of non-Muslims, stating, "There is to be no compulsion in religion," and the Prophet Muhammad strictly prohibited forced conversions, explaining that Allah considers such belligerent behavior a sin. Moreover, the Prophet taught that to Allah, a forced conversion is worthless—a person who converts to Islam because he fears for his life remains a non-Muslim. In practice, however, pagans were often given the choice of converting to Islam or being put to death. Jews and Christians living in areas conquered by the Islamic armies were permitted to continue their religious practices without converting. However, the Qur'an commanded that non-Muslims who did not wish to convert to Islam (called *dhimmi*) had to pay a protection tax (*jizya*). This tax was assessed on every male non-Muslim living in the Muslim lands; women, children, the elderly, and slaves did not count in assessing the amount of the tax.

Islamic law explains the rationale for the tax. The *jizya* was supposed to be approximately the same amount as the annual tax that Muslims paid, the zakat. By paying the *jizya*, non-Muslims were given a special position in the Muslim state: they enjoyed protection and security.

In addition to the tax, however, the *dhimmi* also had certain obligations to the Muslim state (for example, not to support the enemies of Islam). In return, the caliphs had an obligation to protect the non-Muslims. For example, Umar, the second caliph, returned the tax to the Christian tribes of Palestine when he was unable to defend them against raids by hostile Byzantine forces. Because the caliph could not guarantee their safety, there was no justification for the collection of the tax, and the money had to be returned to the *dhimmi* with the regrets of the Muslim state.

This basic political structure of collecting a tax in return for protection and security was a part of the world order of the time. The taxes paid by the conquered non-Muslims became an important source of funds for the expanding Islamic empire. By 656, less than a quarter of a century after Muhammad's death, the Muslims had conquered most of the Middle East and North Africa.

In that year, the third Islamic caliph, Uthman ibn Affan, was assassinated. Uthman had come to power in 644 after the second caliph was murdered by a Persian prisoner-of-war. As caliph, Uthman was criticized by people who believed his appointments favored members of his family and tribe. Disgruntled Muslims assassinated Uthman and proclaimed Ali bin Ali Talib, Muhammad's son-in-law, the fourth caliph.

Civil war broke out throughout the Islamic world between Ali's followers and those Muslims who did not want him appointed caliph. The war lasted for five years, the entire length of Ali's reign as caliph. Initially, Ali's supporters included a small, extremely conservative group of Muslims, who had developed strict codes of conduct and did not hesitate to expel people from their community or execute those who broke Islamic laws. When Ali tried to make peace with his enemies in 658, this group broke away from his followers, calling themselves Kharijites (from the Arabic word meaning those who secede). In 661, the Kharijites assassinated Ali.

The Sunni-Shiite Split

The murder of Ali ended what came to be known as the era of the "rightly guided" caliphs. It also led to a major division in the Islamic faith. Ali's supporters had always maintained that he was the only legitimate religious leader after the death of Muhammad. They accepted his son Hassan as the second imam, and wanted him to become caliph. However, most of the Muslims rallied behind Ali's main opponent, Muawiyyah ibn Abi Sufyan, who had been a kinsman of the slain third caliph Uthmar.

The larger group of Muslims who supported Muawiyyah became known as the Sunni, which comes from the example set by Muhammad, the Sunna. (The word *sunni* literally means "the path.") Those who followed Ali and his sons became known as Shiites, from the Arabic phrase *Shiat Ali*, meaning "Party of Ali."

As the fifth caliph Muawiyyah managed to reunite the Islamic empire. He moved the capital to Damascus, an ancient city in Syria, because Arabia was no longer the center of political and commercial activity in the Islamic empire. The followers of Ali, meanwhile, backed Hassan's claim to the caliphate until his death in 669, then proclaimed Ali's younger son Hussein the third imam.

Before Muawiyyah died in 680, he appointed his son, Yazid, as the sixth caliph. Muawiyyah did this because he wanted to ensure a smooth succession of rulers and avoid another civil war. However, some Muslims opposed Yazid because they wanted the caliphate to remain an elected office, rather than a hereditary one. Civil war erupted again, as Hussein's supporters claimed that he was the rightful caliph. However, Yazid's army slaughtered Hussein and a group of his followers at the Battle of Karbala.

The death of Hussein marked the end of Shiite power in the Islamic state. Since then, the Shiites have traditionally been a minority group. Today more than 80 percent of the worldwide Muslim population is Sunni, while less than 15 percent are Shiites.

However, the Battle of Karbala did not end the fighting. The civil war continued until 691, as various Muslim leaders fought over the caliphate. Kharijites tried to establish an independent Arab state. Finally, a Umayyad caliph named Abd al-Mailk was able to restore order to the empire. His son, al-Walid, became caliph in 705.

Despite these decades of turmoil, Islam continued to spread throughout the Middle East. By the time al-Walid became caliph, Muslim armies ruled all of North Africa, the Middle East, and Persia, and were raiding across the Mediterranean Sea into Europe. By 718 the Iberian Peninsula—modern-day Spain and Portugal—was under Islamic rule, and Islamic forces had moved into Afghanistan and central Asia.

The Islamic Influence on Europe

During the eighth and ninth centuries the spread of Islam was driven by much more than military conquest. The enlightened Islamic culture was attractive to many people, particularly when compared to the repressive—and at times barbaric—systems of thought that had prevailed in the Byzantine and Persian empires. Trade and the exchange of goods and ideas played a more central role in the spread of the religion than did warfare, particularly as Islam spread into Asia.

As the Islamic world expanded, large numbers of people converted to the new religion. Many people found Islam to be an attractive alternative

This fresco shows Shiites killed at the Battle of Karbala in CE 680. The massacre of Hussein and many of his followers established the Umayyads as rulers of the Muslims.

to their old beliefs. Others recognized that conversion would release them from their obligations as *dhimmis* and give them greater rights in the Islamic society, which by this time dominated the region.

The Muslim world endured another civil war from 744 to 750. The war ended when the Abbasids, members of a family that was descended from an uncle of Muhammad, defeated the Umayyads and established a new ruling dynasty that would last for the next several centuries. The Abbasids moved their capital to Baghdad, in present-day Iraq.

However, the Abbasid rulers lost a piece of their empire soon after it was established—the Islamic territories on the Iberian Peninsula. A member of the Umayyad dynasty, Abd al-Rahman, moved to Spain and established a separate Muslim state there in 756. Concentrating on the southern part of Spain, an area known as Andalusia, the Muslims built the most

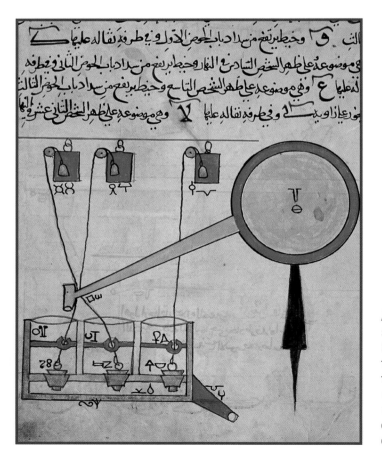

A colorful drawing from an Arabic book shows how a clock utilizes weights to keep accurate time. At the same time that European civilization had fallen into the Dark Ages, Muslim scholars were the most enlightened in the world, and were making great advancements in knowledge of mathematics, astronomy, science, geography, and other subjects.

enlightened civilization in Europe during the eighth and ninth centuries. The major Muslim city in Spain, Córdoba, witnessed fabulous advances in many areas of art and science. In Andalusia Muslims, Christians, and Jews lived and worked together, exchanging the accumulated knowledge of each of their cultures.

Civilization in Europe had languished before the arrival of the Muslims in the eighth century. The fall of the Roman Empire during the fifth century had plunged Western Europe into a period of decline known as the Dark Ages. During this time much ancient knowledge was lost or destroyed. The only people who received an education were churchmen or members of the landowning nobility, and members of these groups kept tight control over every aspect of European religious, business, political, artistic, and social life. The great majority of people living in Europe were uneducated peasants, who eked out a meager living on small farms and in scattered communities and had no opportunity to educate themselves or improve their situation in life.

By contrast, the Muslims were familiar with the rich cultures of the lands they had conquered. Ancient Greek and Roman writings that had been lost or destroyed in Europe during the Dark Ages had been preserved in Eastern libraries and translated into Arabic, and Muslim geographers, astronomers, and scientists built on this ancient knowledge. On the Iberian Peninsula, cities like Córdoba and Toledo became important centers for the exchange of culture and ideas. In Andalusia the people of Europe were exposed to advanced mathematics, science, medicine, and philosophy, as well as a wide range of technical, agricultural, and artistic skills. This cultural exchange would help bring Europe out of the Dark Ages.

At the same time Islam was spreading into Europe from the East as well. The rule of the Abbasids continued to grow until their territory stretched across North Africa to Sicily and Greece, and from the Middle East into northern India. During the ninth century, the Islamic empire ruled by the Abbasids was larger than the Roman Empire had been at its height.

Like the Muslim cities of Andalusia, Muslim cities under Abbasid rule also played an important role in the cultural exchange between Islam and the West. Students from Europe attended schools in Cairo, Damascus,

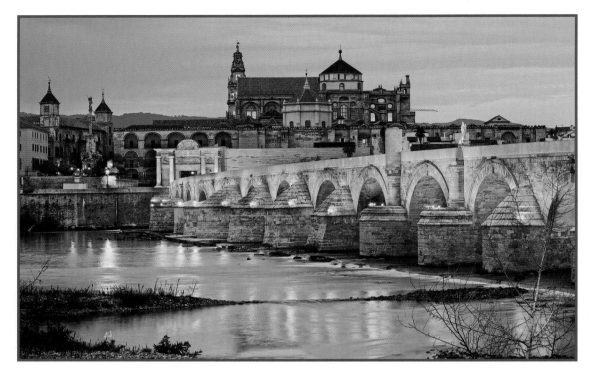

The mosque of Córdoba overlooks the Guadlquvir River, Andalusia, Spain. Muslims had a great influence on the Iberian Peninsula and helped Western Europe emerge from the Dark Ages.

and Baghdad in order to study medicine and the sciences. Sicily also was an important center of learning under Abbasid control. The knowledge that the Muslims had preserved and shared would eventually help bring on the European Renaissance that began in Italy during the 14th century.

Decline of the Islamic States

The Abbasids found it difficult to control their vast empire, and they gradually allowed various regions to withdraw and form self-governing kingdoms. Some of these kingdoms paid monetary tribute to the Abbasids, while others became completely independent. By the tenth century, the Abbasid caliph in Baghdad was merely a figurehead who symbolized Muslim unity, rather than a strong political leader, even though the caliph still controlled parts of the once-vast empire.

During the next few centuries, the Muslim world struggled to reorganize itself. Independent Muslim kingdoms emerged in Iran, Arabia, North Africa, Turkey, and northern India. On the Iberian Peninsula, Christians began fighting against the Muslims in 1002. The European Christians gradually seized land from the Muslim rulers, finally conquering Grenada, the last Muslim stronghold, in 1492.

Though it was no longer appropriate to speak of a united Muslim empire after the tenth century, there was no denying the existence of a Muslim world. A large portion of the global population was firmly committed to the religion that had emerged out of the deserts of Arabia just a few centuries earlier. At the end of the eleventh century, Muslims were drawn into a series of conflicts with Christians that dramatically changed the course of history.

Text-Dependent Questions

1. Who was chosen as the first caliph, or successor to Muhammad?
2. What is the jizya? Why was it assessed?
3. How did Muslims help to bring Europe out of the Medieval period?

Research Project

The division of Islam into Sunni and Shia branches dates back to the seventh century. Using your school library or the Internet, find out more about Ali, Muhammad's son-in-law and companion who became the fourth caliph in 656 ce. Write a two-page report about Ali, and how his assassination in 661 led to the Sunni-Shia split. Include some examples of how these two Muslim sects have clashed throughout history, to the present day.

4

The Crusades

The border between the Christian Byzantine Empire and the empire's Muslim neighbors was always an area of tension. In the eleventh century, a group of Muslims from the western part of modern-day Turkey, the Seljuk Turks, started acquiring power and expanding their territories. Turkish soldiers often raided cities on the Byzantine frontier in order to weaken the empire. In 1095, the Byzantine Emperor Alexios I Komnenos asked the pope, leader of the Roman Catholic Church that held great power over Western Europe, for help fighting the Muslim Turks.

Pope Urban II was eager to help the Byzantine emperor. Earlier in the eleventh century the Christian church had formally split into two sections over a difference in beliefs. Christians in the West, under the leadership of the pope in Rome, became known as Roman Catholics, while Christians in the East were called Orthodox or Eastern Rite Christians. The pope viewed helping the Byzantine emperor as an

Opposite: Christians and Muslims fight fiercely during one of the many Crusades that occurred between 1096 and 1291. The Crusades were a series of wars between invading European Christian armies and the Muslims living in the Middle East. Both sides were fighting over land they considered sacred.

opportunity to reduce the *friction* between Roman Catholics and Orthodox Christians. The pope also had other reasons for wanting to help. Muslims dominated the cities and areas where the most important Christian shrines were located—Jerusalem, the Galilee, and Damascus. The pope wanted Christians to force the Muslims out of these areas and assert Christian rule, so that European believers could go on religious pilgrimages to the holy sites. Finally, many Europeans believed that the Byzantines felt superior to them. The pope and others saw this situation as an opportunity to prove that the Europeans were the equals of the Byzantines.

Pope Urban II called upon the Christians of Europe to fight a holy war, or crusade, against the Muslims. He assigned them two missions. First, they were to help the Byzantine Christians eliminate the Turkish threat from their borders. Second, they were to capture the holy city of Jerusalem, which the Muslims had controlled since the eighth century. As an *incentive*, the pope promised that those who died in battle would have their sins immediately forgiven. People all across Europe willingly responded to the pope's message.

The pope advised the Crusaders to begin their journey after the fall harvest, so that the troops would have enough food to last through the 3,000-mile journey. Approximately 60,000 people from France, Germany, and England who were anxious to get started disregarded the pope's advice and started traveling east in the spring of 1096. This was a very bad decision. Because the crops were not ready for harvesting it was difficult to find food. By the time these Crusaders reached Eastern Europe they were starving. They began robbing farming communities and cities along the way; as a result, the crusading army became involved in battles before it even left Europe. In the area of modern-day Germany, the cru-

📖 Words to Understand in This Chapter

friction—dissension or conflict.

incentive—a thing that motivates or encourages a person to do something.

saders massacred Jews, claiming that they were enemies of the Christian church. In Hungary, the residents grew so angry with the plundering Crusaders that they began to defend their cities as the armies approached. The Crusaders who managed to reach the Byzantine capital, Constantinople, were so weak from hunger that the well-fed and battle-hardened Turkish armies defeated them easily.

This early part of the First Crusade is often called the "Peasants' Crusade." Although many of these Crusaders were peasants, a large number of them were knights. However, even the knights were poorly armed, and they failed primarily because they did not have adequate supplies.

A second group of approximately 100,000 soldiers and pilgrims began their journey east in the fall of 1096. This group of crusaders included the more experienced knights of western Europe, and they came prepared. They had more food and supplies to take with them, so they did not have to forage along the route east. When they arrived at Constantinople, they rested and gathered fresh supplies. In the spring of 1097 the Crusaders set out to battle the Turkish armies. After capturing Nicea, capital of the Seljuk Turks, the Crusaders embarked on a long and difficult campaign down the Mediterranean coast, eventually reaching Jerusalem. When the Christian armies finally broke into the walled city in June 1099, they massacred the Muslims and Jews living there. After sacking Jerusalem, the Crusaders established four small Christian kingdoms along the Mediterranean coast, in the areas of modern-day Israel, Lebanon, and Jordan.

After this some of the Crusaders returned to Europe. Those who remained behind built large castles that they used to defend their kingdoms. Many of these fortresses are still standing. They are particularly interesting because the builders employed a unique blend of European and Arab styles when they erected these structures.

The Second Crusade

The Middle Eastern Crusader states were never completely at peace with their Muslim neighbors. They were small Christian kingdoms surrounded by the Muslims whose land they had taken. Relations between the two groups were complex. To secure their borders, the Crusaders frequently raided and skirmished with the Muslims. They sometimes mistreated Muslims living within their kingdoms. Nonetheless, the Christian settlers also traded with Muslims and intermarried with them.

In 1144 Muslim forces under the command of Imad ad-Din Zengi conquered Edessa, a Crusader state in northern Syria. In response to this news, in 1146 a Roman Catholic priest named Bernard of Clairvaux traveled throughout France and Germany, calling for a Second Crusade. This motivated tens of thousands of people to leave their homes and travel thousands of miles to fight an enemy they did not know.

The political aims of the First Crusade had been to help the Byzantine Empire secure its borders and to bring Jerusalem under Christian control. The political aims of the Second Crusade were to force the Muslims out of Jerusalem, to strengthen the Crusader states, to remove the Muslims from Spain, and to bring western European Christianity to Eastern Europe.

Although Pope Urban II had hoped to bring Roman Catholic and Orthodox Christians together in the First Crusade, this had not happened. At times, the Crusaders had killed Christian Arabs in the Middle East, mistaking them for Muslims. By the time of the Second Crusade, nearly a century had passed since the schism in the Christian Church, and many Roman Catholics believed the Eastern Rite Christians were as misguided in their religious beliefs as the followers of other religions.

King Louis of France and King Conrad of Germany led the armies of the Second Crusade. When the travelers entered the Byzantine Empire Louis maintained discipline among his troops. He did not allow them to abuse the townspeople and farmers. Unfortunately, Conrad did not maintain such order, and his troops robbed and mistreated the Orthodox Christians. Their disrespect for the Byzantine citizens further strained the relations between eastern and western Europeans.

King Conrad grew ill before the Crusaders reached the Middle East and had to return to Europe. This left King Louis in charge of the Crusader army. King Louis was a devoutly religious man, not a military leader, and the Muslims defeated the Crusaders easily. The embarrassed Crusaders returned to Europe, leaving the small Crusader states more vulnerable than they had been before.

The remains of the Crusader sea castle in Sidon, Lebanon, a stronghold of one of the Crusader kingdoms established in the region. The Crusaders captured Sidon in 1111 and held the city almost continuously until 1291. After the Muslims wiped out the Crusader kingdoms, the castles were destroyed to prevent Europeans from regaining another foothold in the region.

A Century of Warfare, 1190–1291

Within a few decades, the Muslims, under the leadership of the great Kurdish general Saladin, began to recapture cities from the Christians, including Jerusalem in 1187. In response, Pope Gregory VIII called for a Third Crusade. The response was less enthusiastic this time, and the armies of the Third Crusade did not sail for the Middle East until 1190.

The response was slow in part because France and England were fighting each other. The Crusade could not begin until England's King Richard and France's King Philip reached a truce. After England and France settled their differences, their armies sailed to the Holy Land. (A powerful army from Germany, which was ruled by Emperor Frederick I, also set out on the Crusade, but after Frederick died during the journey most of his army returned to Germany.)

One of the major sieges of the Third Crusade occurred at the city of Acre on the Mediterranean coast. The French forces arrived first; the English army under Richard had stopped to capture Cyprus, an island in the Mediterranean Sea, in order to protect the Crusader supply lines. After the English army arrived, the Crusaders prevented food and supplies from being brought into Acre and began to dig tunnels under the walls of the city so they would collapse. With its food supply exhausted and its walls weakened by the Crusaders, Acre was forced to surrender in July 1191.

The English King Richard (sometimes remembered as Richard the Lionhearted) has a positive reputation in the West as a brave and chivalrous knight. Muslims, however, remember him best for something that happened after the fall of Acre—the massacre of nearly 3,000 Muslim prisoners on a hill called Ayyadieh outside the city. This action earned him the nickname "the Butcher of Ayyadieh" among the Muslims.

After the fall of Acre, Philip returned to France. Richard, however, continued marching along the coast toward Jerusalem. Although he won an important victory at Jaffa in 1192, his army was not strong enough to capture Jerusalem. Instead, the Christian and Muslim armies became locked in a stalemate. After several months, Richard and Saladin negotiated a five-year truce that stabilized the borders between the Christians and Muslims. The Muslims would retain control of Jerusalem, but unarmed Christian pilgrims would be permitted to visit the holy city without fear of being attacked.

Even though Richard did not recapture Jerusalem, he had gained some peace and stability for the weak Crusader kingdoms. Nevertheless, many Europeans considered the Third Crusade a failure. In 1199 a group of noblemen from France and Belgium persuaded a new pope, Innocent III, to sponsor a fourth crusade. However, in Venice these crusaders became entangled in complex political and commercial schemes. The Venetians diverted the crusading armies from the Holy Land to Constantinople, where an ambitious prince, Alexius, was trying to take over his father's throne. Alexius enlisted the Crusaders to assist him and he became co-emperor alongside of his father. The armies of the Fourth Crusade stayed in Constantinople with Alexius—they never reached the Holy Land.

In 1204, a group of rebels strangled Alexius. His father died just a few days later. The rebels crowned a new emperor and tried to force the Crusaders out of the city. The French knights felt that the only way to restore stability to the Byzantine empire—and keep themselves safe in Constantinople—was to appoint one of their own leaders as the new emperor. This led to a conflict that the Crusaders ended by sacking Constantinople. These events caused a final breakdown of relations between the Eastern and Western branches of the Christian church.

A manuscript illustration shows the coronation of Richard I (1157–1199) as king of England. Richard was nicknamed Coeur de Lion (Lionhearted) because of his bravery and skill in battle, and he is often depicted in Western history as a noble and valiant leader. In reality, however, Richard was a brutal and ruthless warrior and ruler.

By this time, also, many Europeans were losing interest in crusading. Pope Innocent III called for a Fifth Crusade shortly before he died in 1216, but his successor, Honorious III, had a hard time enlisting people to fight. The Christians living in the Middle East did not want a new crusade to begin either. The Bishop of Acre asked the pope not to send any more soldiers to the Holy Land because the Crusader kingdoms were building good relations with their Muslim neighbors. They did not want knights from Europe coming and wrecking the peace.

Nevertheless, a small crusading army landed in Egypt in 1218. The Crusaders and the Muslims fought to a stalemate. Some of the Crusaders thought it was possible to convince the Muslims to become Christians. They began preaching to the Egyptian Muslims, and some converted to Christianity. Eventually, however, the Muslim armies defeated the Crusaders and forced them to leave Egypt in 1221.

Frederick II, emperor of Germany and Sicily, began assembling the armies of the Sixth Crusade in 1227. He wanted to conquer the Middle East because his dream was to be like Alexander the Great. Frederick was one of the most educated men in Europe at this time, and was fluent in nine languages. Even though he was a Christian he respected Islam and had many Muslim advisers. In 1229, Frederick negotiated a treaty that established Christian rule in Jerusalem and some neighboring cities for a ten-year period. The Muslims would evacuate the city, but they would be able to return as pilgrims to worship at their holy places. Frederick was crowned as the King of Jerusalem, but the peace did not last. Muslims and Christians throughout the region objected to the treaty. Neither side wanted to give anything to the other without a fight, and Frederick ultimately returned home empty-handed.

King Louis IX of France led the seventh and final crusade in 1248. Louis was an extremely devout Christian, not a soldier. His inept military leadership led to his army's capture in Egypt. Louis negotiated a peace treaty and returned home with his the remains of his army in 1254.

The weak Crusader states survived until 1291, when in a final offensive the Muslims forced out the Christians and regained the rest of the territory they had lost nearly 200 years earlier. Some minor crusading adventures continued for another two centuries but these were ineffective.

Ultimately, the European efforts to conquer the Middle East in God's name were tragic and wasteful.

"Holy War" versus Jihad

The ferocity of the Crusaders horrified Muslims. The massacre in Jerusalem in 1099, during which the Christian Crusaders killed Muslim and Jewish men, women, and children, is one of the most appalling episodes in history. The people living in the Middle East desperately defended their homes against these vicious invaders for nearly two centuries.

During the Crusades, Muslims and Christians developed specific ideas to justify the wars they fought. The Christian notion of "holy war" and the Muslim concept of "jihad" were used to explain, excuse, and inspire the fighting.

The Christian holy war was conceived as a means of purification. This involved two distinct processes. First, anything or anyone not totally dedicated to God had to be destroyed or purified. From the Christian point of view, the Muslims were impure and had to be destroyed. Christians also believed that the presence of Muslims in the Holy Land made that place impure. They had to force the Muslims out of the Holy Land and return it to God's people—the Christians. This point of view is consistent with Old Testament accounts of the Israelite conquest of Canaan. These stories tell how God commanded his people to clean out the land by destroying everyone in it, and to settle there themselves.

Also, Christians believed that fighting a war for God purified them and made them better Christians. The hardships they endured made them humble and dependent on God's grace. Death on the battlefield ensured special places for them in heaven as defenders of the faith. To die a martyr's death was to gain glorious entry to eternal paradise. Suffering and death, especially during a holy war, were ways to achieve personal purity.

During the Fifth Crusade, some Christians began developing the idea that converting their enemies would purify them, and would be an acceptable alternative to destroying them. This idea comes from the ancient practice of using fire to purify precious metals, which is mentioned in the Old Testament. If one removes all impurities from an object, that object can be used in God's service. Some of the Christians thought they should persuade the Muslims to turn away from their "impure" religion and follow the "pure" faith of Christianity.

All of these ideas were embodied in the Christian concept of holy war. The Muslim notion of jihad is quite different from this Christian idea. The word *jihad* literally means "struggle." In Islam, the greater jihad refers to one's personal struggle to live a moral life. The lesser jihad refers to warfare. In Muslim thinking, personal jihad is more sacred than political or military jihad.

In Islamic law, jihad is intimately tied to the notion of the restoration of rights. Jihad is a struggle to maintain the balance of justice by a fair and equitable distribution of rights and duties. This is why the Prophet Muhammad taught that if a person defends his home or property against a thief or aggressor, he or she is engaged in a jihad.

During the Muslim expansion of the seventh and eighth centuries, some Muslims taught that a world created and ruled by one God should be united under one religion. Some of the early wars of this era were fought to achieve that goal. Within a few decades, however, the Muslims formulated and applied a policy under which they could peacefully coexist with Christians and Jews.

The Qur'an condemns aggressive warfare and commands Muslims to fight only in self-defense. However, the Qur'an explicitly states that "self-defense" includes fighting against oppression or the denial of basic rights. Jihad is legitimate when it is targeted at ending oppression and restoring justice, as long as the Muslim does not commit an injustice in the name of seeking justice. Today, the Muslim idea of self-defense has expanded to include resisting any social or cultural influences that contradict Muslim teachings and practices.

The Crusades were a crucial factor in the development of the West's self-image and ideals. The word "crusade" stimulates positive feelings in Westerners, who often use the word to refer to an effort to improve something—a "crusade against injustice," for example. The word is used this way because the primarily Christian West has traditionally viewed the Crusades as a positive venture. Legends have always portrayed Crusader heroes like Richard the Lionhearted in a positive way, and downplayed the bloody reality of the Crusaders' exploits.

The Muslim response to the word "crusade" differs dramatically. The word makes Muslims think of invasion, aggression, and brutality. Some Muslims hear the word "crusade" as a call to arms that is specifically directed against them. In the week after the September 11, 2001, terrorist attacks against the United States, President George W. Bush commented that "this crusade, this war on terrorism, is going to take a while." This remark attracted little attention in the United States, but inadvertently offended some Muslims because of its negative historical connotations.

Many contemporary Muslims see the Crusades as a key to understanding Muslim relations with the West. They perceive a direct connection between the European belligerence of the Middle Ages and Western involvement in Muslim lands in the modern age.

 # Text-Dependent Questions

1. What two missions did Pope Urban II assign to the Crusaders in 1095? What reward did he promise to those who participated?

2. What occurred on a hill called Ayyadieh outside the city of Acre in 1191?

3. When were the last of the Crusader states overrun by Muslim armies?

 # Research Project

Modern historians say that there were at least seven major Crusades, as well as some minor fighting, between 1096 to 1291. Choose one of the major crusades and find out more about it, using the Internet or your school library. What were the major battles? Who were the leaders on each side? What were the military aims of the Crusade, and what strategies did the leaders use to accomplish those goals? Write a two-page report about the Crusade and present what you've found to your class.

5

Islamic and European Empires

As the fervor for crusading was fading in Europe, Muslims found themselves facing a new danger from the east. Throughout the thirteenth century much of the Muslim world's attention was directed toward a far more frightening group of invaders—the Mongols.

The Mongols came from an area north of China called Mongolia. They began building their empire by conquering much of China. They traveled westward and began invading Muslim countries in southern and central Asia in 1220. Under the leadership of Genghis Khan they pursued their goal of establishing a worldwide empire.

The Mongols were interested in conquest, not culture. As they swept east through Asia, Mongol armies obliterated cities, burned hundreds of libraries, and killed thousands of people. The Mongols terrified all who fought them. In 1258 the Mongols *sacked* Baghdad. The city, which had long been an important center of

Opposite: In the centuries that followed the Crusades, new Muslim empires emerged. One of the most glorious of these was the Moghul Empire, based in India. The Moghul emperor Shah Jehan built the Taj Mahal as a tomb for his wife. It was completed in 1648 and is considered one of the most beautiful buildings ever built.

Islamic culture and learning, was destroyed, and most of the inhabitants were slaughtered. (According to some accounts, the Mongol leader Hülegü Khan, grandson of Genghis Khan, made a pyramid from the skulls of poets, scholars, and religious leaders in Baghdad.) By 1260, the Mongol empire stretched from China to the Mediterranean Sea.

Despite this invasion, Islamic culture remained dominant in a large portion of the world. (The Mongols themselves would make Islam their official religion in 1313.) Islam spread throughout a huge area, including China, sub-Saharan Africa, India, Malaysia, and Indonesia—the lands that today are home to a majority of the world's Muslim population—without major battles or military conquests. This was primarily the result of commercial relations, as Muslims from the Middle East and central Asia established thriving trade relations with merchants from China, India, and the eastern and northern coasts of Africa. Most Muslims of this period looked toward Asia, rather than Europe, for commercial and cultural exchange. They believed Europeans were crude and uncivilized.

Rise of the Ottoman Empire

One group of Muslims did maintain continuous contact with Europeans, Asians, and Africans, however: the Ottoman Turks, founders of the remarkable Ottoman empire. Under the leadership of Osman I (1259–1326), the Ottoman Turks removed the Seljuk Turks from power and established the foundations of a new empire.

As Ottoman strength grew, the Turks began expanding their area of control. They conquered Syria and Egypt, then began chipping away at the edges of the Byzantine empire. In 1453, the Ottoman Turks succeeded in sacking Constantinople, bringing the thousand-year-old Byzantine

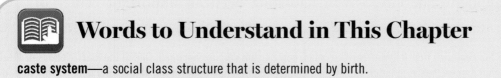

Words to Understand in This Chapter

caste system—a social class structure that is determined by birth.

sack—to plunder and destroy a captured city or other place.

This artwork from a Persian manuscript depicts the sack of Baghdad, an important city in the Arab Muslim empire, in 1258. As the Abbasid empire disintegrated, other powerful empires would take its place in the Islamic world.

empire to an end. The Turks changed the name of the city to Istanbul (which means "city of Islam"), and made it their capital.

One effect of the Ottoman takeover of the Byzantine lands was that many Christian scholars and artists moved to Italy. These refugees contributed to the intellectual and artistic renaissance that had started there in the 14th century and was spreading across Europe.

The Ottoman Turks used the doctrine of jihad to justify their conquests of both Muslims and non-Muslims by declaring themselves the defenders of Islam. As defenders of Islam, the Ottomans were responsible for ensuring that all Muslims practiced pure Islam. This justified their taking control of neighboring Muslims countries. As defenders of Islam, the Ottomans had a duty to proclaim the message of Islam to non-Muslims. They also had to ensure safe passages for all Muslims on their annual pilgrimages to Mecca. These grounds justified attacks on their non-Muslim neighbors.

Even though the Ottomans were Muslims they allowed the people they conquered to continue practicing their own religions. These non-Muslims, mostly Christians, were called *millets*. The Ottomans also invited Jews to live in the empire. Many Jews accepted this invitation because the Ottomans generally treated them more humanely than the Europeans did.

The Ottoman ruler, or sultan, was the supreme director of the government, head of the military, and religious leader of Islam. He held all of the power in the empire. The sultan had the final decision in all matters brought to him, and his decisions could not be overruled. The sultan was expected to use his power to guarantee justice to everyone in the empire. The Ottomans were great lawmakers, and they built complex legal institutions. The sultan also upheld very strict laws against government and military corruption. Tax collectors and other government officials who treated people unfairly or accepted bribes received severe punishment—the death penalty was common in such cases.

The Ottomans also promoted an effective government by promoting talented people to important positions. Unlike in other empires and systems of government, high-ranking positions had to be earned, not inherited—even the sultanate, to a degree. The member of the royal family judged as the most fit to rule became the sultan. In some cases, other male members of the sultan's family were then either executed or imprisoned so that there would not be power struggles between rival princes.

The empire flourished in part because of its government system, and in part because of the development of a well-educated and well-trained army and an effective network of spies. The Ottoman army was one of the first to use gunpowder for military purposes. An important corps of soldiers was composed almost entirely of slaves who were fanatically loyal to the sultan. Government spies regularly traveled throughout the empire and reported their findings to the sultan and his administrators. The Ottomans maintained the world's most effective spy network until the empire's collapse after World War I.

The Ottoman empire reached its greatest glory during the long reign of Sultan Suleiman, between 1520 and 1566. The Muslims called him

"Suleiman the Lawgiver" because he developed a comprehensive set of laws that he enforced throughout the vast empire. Scholarship and art flourished during this period, and Suleiman himself was considered one the finest poets in the world. During his rule, one of the greatest architects in history, Sinan, designed many impressive mosques, bridges, and palaces. His Sulemaniye Mosque still dominates the skyline of Istanbul, and of the 477 buildings constructed by Sinan, 196 are still standing.

Suleiman was admired throughout his empire, which during his rule included lands in southeastern Europe, such as present-day Greece, Macedonia, Bulgaria, Romania, and Hungary. He was well known around the world; Europeans called him "Suleiman the Magnificent." In

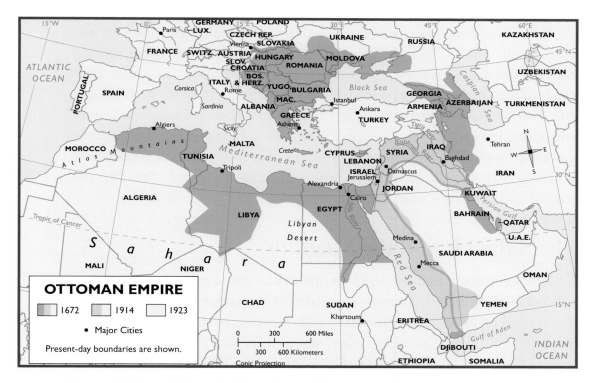

The powerful Ottoman Turks controlled one of the world's greatest empires. At its height in 1672, the Ottoman empire controlled a large part of eastern Europe, northern Africa, and the Middle East. However, by the start of World War I in 1914, the empire had been reduced by the encroachment of European powers and weakened by internal corruption. The Treaty of Lausanne, signed in July 1923, established the borders of modern-day Turkey. The former Ottoman territories were divided among the victorious allied powers, particularly France and Great Britain.

1529 his army surrounded Vienna, the capital of Austria, but failed to capture the city. However, Austria and Russia continued to feel threatened by the Ottomans during the next two centuries.

After Suleiman's death the empire continued to grow in size, but its power slowly declined. One reason was that many sultans took over leadership of the empire without first receiving any training. They spent their youths in imprisoned isolation, then suddenly were expected to rule an empire that engaged in complex international political, commercial, and military relationships. The inability of the sultans to provide skilled leadership enabled government and military leaders to become selfish and corrupt. Government positions were no longer earned by ability, they were sold to the families that paid the most for them. Accordingly, the overall quality of the empire's administration fell sharply.

While the Ottoman empire was suffering its leadership crisis in the seventeenth century, the countries of Europe were building their military and commercial strength. As European empires grew stronger, they expanded into the fringes of the Ottoman empire. In wars with Russia and Austria, the Ottomans lost their European territory. Ottomans power and influence continued to wane as the rising European powers slowly picked it apart. By the nineteenth century the once-glorious empire was ridiculed throughout the West as "the sick man of Europe." Finally, the empire was dissolved after the end of World War I.

The Safavids and the Moghuls

Two other strong Muslim empires appeared in the sixteenth century. The Safavid empire included Persia and parts of Turkey and Georgia. Before the Safavids gained power in 1501 most Muslims in this region followed Sunni Islam. The Safavids, who were Shiite Muslims, aggressively imposed Shiism on the people they conquered. This changed the way these people practiced Islam. In addition to the usual celebrations of Ramadan and the Hajj (the pilgrimage to Mecca), the Safavid Shiites encouraged the celebration of Ashura. This time of mourning commemorates the death of Ali's son Hussein in 680. Shiite Muslims in Iran still observe this event.

The Safavid capital was located in the city of Isfahan, which is still one of the world's most beautiful cities. Architectural highlights of the city include dozens of bridges, mosques, and religious shrines. Some of these were built as early as the tenth century. Safavid artists made great innovations in metalworking, and in visual and textile arts. People around the world still regard Persian miniature paintings and carpets as great treasures.

The Safavid empire survived for just over two centuries. In 1722 the empire was torn apart by internal disputes. Although Persia remained a large and powerful force in the region, it became closely allied with a European power, Great Britain. In 1979, more than 250 years after the fall of the Safavids, the Persian people would still be struggling with many of the religious, social, and political issues that had destroyed the mighty Safavid empire.

Descendants of the Mongols established the Moghul empire in India in 1526. One notable feature of this kingdom was the establishment of peaceful relations between its many religious groups—Muslims, Hindus, Buddhists, Christians, Jews, and others. Muslims ruled the Moghul empire, but maintained a policy of religious tolerance as the Qur'an commands. The Muslim rulers made up just a small percentage of the population of the Moghul empire, so religious intolerance easily could have led to their overthrow. Also, India already had a longstanding tradition of religious tolerance. India's social structure was based on a *caste system* in which each social class had its own religious traditions. People were allowed to practice a wide range of religions as long as they respected the rigid social class structure.

Like the Safavid empire, the Moghul empire left a rich cultural heritage. Moghul rulers built a strong central system of government and encouraged painting, gardening, and architecture.

The Moghul empire began to fail in the early years of the eighteenth century when a Moghul emperor named Aurangzeb tried to impose religious uniformity throughout the empire. This policy led to a revolt by the Hindu majority. The Moghuls were greatly weakened by this conflict, and gradually lost control of India to Great Britain in the late 18th century.

The Ottomans, Safavids, and Moghuls were three great Islamic empires. Their downfalls were caused to some degree by internal divisions and weaknesses. Another factor in their demise was the rise of European powers, and their eventual involvement in the Muslim world.

The Rise of European Colonialism

Until the sixteenth century the Ottoman empire held firm control over all of the overland trade routes that led from Europe to Africa and Asia. Merchants from France or England, for example, had to travel across Europe and through the Ottoman empire in order to conduct business in India and China. Even if they sailed across the Mediterranean Sea they eventually had to pass through the Ottoman empire to continue eastward. These journeys took a long time and could be dangerous. They were also

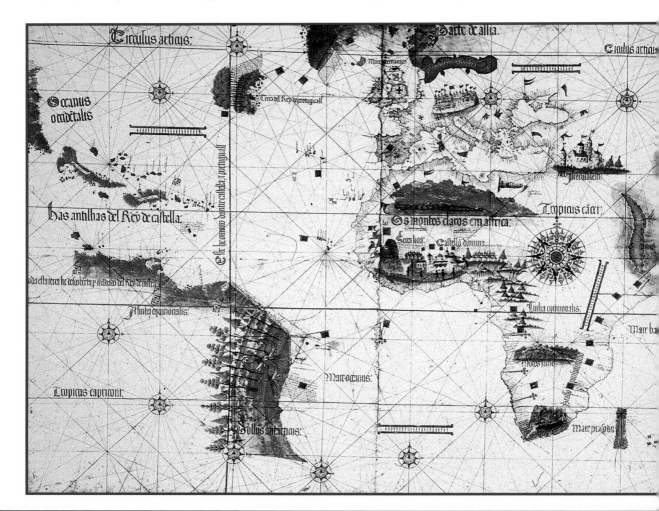

expensive because the Ottomans charged high taxes to merchants passing through their lands. Merchants all over Europe wanted to find cheaper, faster ways to travel to the Far East. They looked to the seas for solutions to their problems.

Some of the early European explorers—particularly the Portuguese—sailed around the coast of Africa into the Indian Ocean. From there, they sailed to India and China. Others—like Christopher Columbus, John Cabot, and Ferdinand Magellan—sailed west in search of the Indies. Columbus explored the Caribbean and the coast of South America during his four voyages, Cabot sailed to North America, and Magellan found a passage through South America and reached the Philippines. These voyages of discovery were very dangerous—both Cabot and Magellan died

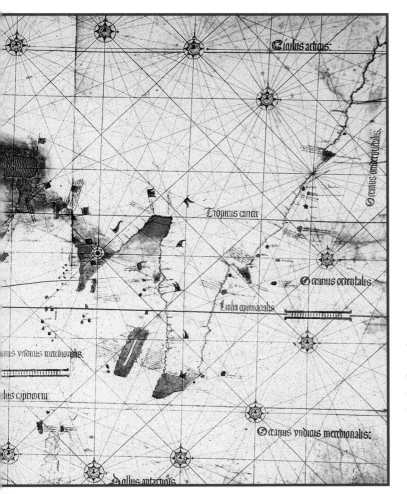

This Portuguese map of the world, drawn in 1501, shows Portuguese possessions in the New World (Brazil), along the coasts of Africa, and in the Middle East and Asia. European countries fought for control over territories all over the world, and imposed their rule on the people living there.

on their journeys—but exploration was believed to be worth the risks, because a great deal of money could be made through trade with the East.

As the European powers learned more about North and South America, the rulers of such countries as Spain, France, England, Portugal, and the Netherlands hurried to seize control of the territory. Through wars and treaties, the Europeans divided the continents among themselves. They did this without regard for the indigenous people who had lived there long before the arrival of Columbus. As European colonies were established, millions of Native Americans were slaughtered, enslaved, or forced to move to new areas in order to make room for the conquerors. European influences still dominate the cultures of both continents.

While these things were happening in the western hemisphere, Austria and Russia continued struggling against the Ottoman empire for lands in Eastern Europe and central Asia. Eventually, the other European powers turned to the East as well, looking for new lands to bring into their growing colonial empires.

Although in the 16th and 17th centuries most Muslims still believed Europeans were crude barbarians, this was no longer true. In Europe during the Renaissance, great advances had been made in science and technology—often by building upon discoveries originally made by Muslims. The Muslims had grown accustomed to thinking of themselves as the givers of civilization, and they paid little attention to European ideas and technology. They rarely adapted European ideas or technology for their own purposes. As a result, Europe was able to use its more sophisticated technology to gain advantage over the rest of the world.

Throughout the sixteenth and seventeenth centuries, powerful European countries forced the weaker Muslim rulers into a series of preferential trade agreements. Nevertheless, the balance of international power did not shift decisively to Europe until the eighteenth and nineteenth centuries. The industrial revolution in Europe gave western countries the advantage they needed to dominate international commerce. After the industrial revolution, the Europeans overwhelmed the less-developed people living in the rest of the world, and forced extensive social, religious, and political changes everywhere they did business.

The Portuguese were the first European power to arrive in the Middle East, and they used force to capture African, Arab, Persian, and Indian ports from which Portuguese warships could protect their trading vessels. During the 17th century, Great Britain and the Netherlands sent their own militaries into the Persian Gulf region to wrest control away from the Portuguese. The British soon became the most dominant of the European colonial powers.

A major step in the European domination of the Muslim world was taken when the British brought India into their empire. This process began in 1765 when the British East India Company, a trading association that was closely connected to the British government, forced the weak Moghul emperor of India to yield his authority. By the middle of the nineteenth century the British controlled all of India (including the area of modern-day Pakistan). The British also expanded their influence into other lands that are primarily Muslim, such as Egypt, Sudan, and the small Arab kingdoms along the Persian Gulf. One of the main reasons Britain became involved in the Middle East was to protect its shipping route to and from India.

But Britain was not the only colonial power during the eighteenth and nineteenth centuries. Russia exerted influence over much of central Asia. Portugal maintained colonies on the West African coast. The Netherlands controlled Java, Borneo, and several islands in the East Indies. France colonized most of north and west Africa, while Italy controlled Libya and Somaliland. The United States acquired territories in Puerto Rico, the Philippines, Hawaii, and Alaska. By the beginning of the twentieth century much of the world was controlled by these imperial powers.

The 1884 Berlin West Africa Conference can be seen as an example of how colonial powers divided land among themselves without the consent of the people whom they presumed to govern, or without anticipating the consequences of their actions beyond extending their own power and influence. At the conference, fourteen European nations—including Great Britain, France, Belgium, Portugal, Italy, Germany, and Spain—divided Africa into various colonial areas under European rule. They did this without consulting with any Africans, simply assuming that the continent and the world was theirs to do with as they wished. The Europeans created about fifty new "countries" by imposing geographic boundaries over the more than a thousand different people and cultures of Africa. Often, these countries included groups of people who did not get along.

European domination over colonial possessions had a devastating effect on Muslim culture. The colonial powers often demanded trading concessions from the territories they ruled, which enabled them to take resources from the lands to maintain the strength of their empires. These colonial policies caused much resentment and anger among the Muslim population.

The White Man's Burden

The observation that Western technology was superior to that of non-Western countries led many Westerners to believe that they were superior to the colonized people. Consequently, Westerners imposed their religious, social, and political practices on the people they colonized. They believed that by doing so they were improving the lives of their colonial subjects. The French believed they had a mission to civilize their colonies, and the British spoke of the burden of imperialism—sometimes called the "white man's burden."

An element of the "white man's burden" was that the imperial powers were supposed to show the people of their colonies the benefits of democracy. Unfortunately, this rarely happened. Democracy was not taught or established in the colonies, and most people had little say in government. This led many Muslims to distrust Western claims about democracy, and to view the colonial powers as using democracy as an excuse to impose Western hegemony and dominance. That this distrust remains was clearly illustrated in 2003, when many Muslims opposed the US invasion of Iraq, which was undertaken in the name of overthrowing Saddam Hussein's dictatorship and bringing democracy to the country.

The colonizers frequently worked with local leaders in the areas they colonized. Many of these leaders were educated in Western universities, where they acquired Western ways of thinking and behaving. Traditional Muslim economic systems were torn apart and rebuilt according to Western norms. Independent artisans and merchants were replaced by factories that provided cheap labor and goods for their colonial masters. Schoolteachers were compelled to teach Western ideas and beliefs and to ignore their native traditions. People who wore traditional clothing rather than Western fashions were ridiculed. Although the colonized people were permitted to practice their traditional religions, colonial governments openly supported Christian missionaries who aggressively sought converts.

As Muslims and Westerners came into closer contact, Islamic societies were constantly pressured to change. For hundreds of years during the Middle Ages, Muslim scholars had dominated the studies of philosophy, science, art, and architecture. Muslims led the world in developing new ideas and perfecting old ones. By the twentieth century, however, Western philosophical, artistic, and scientific ideas overshadowed those of the Muslim world.

Some Muslim leaders wanted to find ways to adopt Western technology and ideas, while still remaining faithful to their heritage. One idea

In 1765 the Moghul emperor Shah Alum gave Robert Clive of the British East India Company permission to administer most of India and collect government revenues. This eventually led to India becoming part of the British empire. It remained an important British colony until after World War II.

was to integrate the best aspects of Islam with the best features of the West. This attitude was particularly popular in the nineteenth century. Some tried to merge Muslim and Western democratic ideals. Others tried to merge Muslim ideals with socialism or communism. In its later years, the Ottoman empire tried to adapt modern technology while maintaining an autocratic, Islamic-based government.

Reshaping the Islamic World

In such countries as India and Egypt, the Muslim populations chafed against their European colonial rulers during the late nineteenth and early twentieth centuries. However, even in the territories ruled by the Ottoman sultan—who was still considered the Islamic caliph—part of the Muslim population was beginning to question their rulers' authority. In the Arab countries under Ottoman dominance, a nationalist movement was beginning to develop.

Nationalism—the desire for political independence by a people with a separate identity and culture but no state of their own—grew slowly. The Arabs had always been more tightly bound by family and tribal connections; the idea of a nation-state (a country made up of people with similar ethnic or cultural characteristics) was considered a Western concept. Intellectuals and military leaders who had been educated in the West formed the first groups that promoted nationalism in the Ottoman empire.

Arab nationalism grew out of an effort by some Turkish officials to remove the Ottoman Sultan Abdul Hamid. The Ottoman Committee of Union and Progress promoted a constitutional reform of the government, and promised autonomy to the Arabs and other groups that lived under Ottoman rule. However, after the sultan was forced from power in 1908, Arabs were disappointed to find that the committee's reforms involved placing Turkish culture in a primary position throughout the Ottoman empire, rather than permitting Arab autonomy.

In cities like Cairo, Beirut, and Damascus, some educated Arabs formed secret organizations to work for Arab freedom from the Ottoman Empire. These included the Ottoman Decentralization Party, Al Ahd (The Covenant Society), and Al Fatat (The Young Arabs). However, comparatively few Arabs supported the nationalist ideas proposed by these groups.

While unrest continued in the Ottoman empire, in Europe the imperial powers were preparing for war. The conflict, which began in August 1914, pitted the Central Powers (Germany, Austria-Hungary, and the Ottoman empire) against the Allied Powers (Britain, France, and Russia). The scope of the conflict quickly spread beyond Europe, however. The First World War became global because the major participants were involved in so many parts of the world.

With Britain and the Ottoman empire on opposite sides of the conflict, British envoys like T. E. Lawrence were sent to the Middle East to encourage the Arabs to fight against Ottoman rule. The British appealed to the idea of Arab nationalism by promising the creation of an independent Arab state if the Ottomans were defeated. In June 1916, Hussein bin Ali, the sharif of Mecca, declared the Arab revolt. During the war Arab forces worked with British and French troops to capture important cities such as Damascus and Aleppo. However, the revolt involved only a small percentage of the total Arab population; most Arabs did not become involved in the revolt, and some fought enthusiastically as part of the Ottoman armies.

However, at the same time Britain was encouraging the Arab revolt, its diplomats were also meeting secretly with French leaders to divide the Ottoman territories between them. The Sykes-Picot agreement, signed in May 1916, provided a plan to separate Arab lands into small states—each of which would be under French or British rule. In addition, in 1917 the British foreign secretary, Arthur James Lord Balfour, wrote to a Jewish leader, Lord Rothshild, assuring him that the British government supported the idea of creating a homeland for the Jews in Palestine. The British hoped this "Balfour Declaration" would help them win Jewish support for the Allied cause. Arabs, however, felt betrayed.

When the First World War ended in 1918, the victorious Allied powers established neither an Arab nor a Jewish state in Palestine. Instead, the newly formed League of Nations, an international organization created so that nations could work peacefully to resolve issues and problems, gave France and Britain mandates to rule the territories taken from the Ottoman empire. These territories were broken into new states or regions:

The Council of Four allied leaders—David Lloyd George of Great Britain, Vittorio Orlando of Italy, Georges Clemenceau of France, and Woodrow Wilson of the United States—meet in May 1919 during the Paris Peace Conference. During the first six months of 1919, the victorious allies carved the former Ottoman territories into a collection of new states, most under British or French control. This redrawing of the world map set the stage for regional conflicts throughout the 20th century.

Transjordan, Palestine, Syria, Lebanon, and Iraq. The stated intention of the League's mandate system was for the western powers to help these newly created states build democratic governments. In reality, however, these mandates essentially became colonial dependencies.

Even states like Egypt, which became independent in 1922, remained strongly influenced by British rule. Great Britain also maintained close ties to many of the Gulf States, such as Kuwait, Oman, and the Trucial States (a collection of small kingdoms that include the present-day nations of Bahrain, Qatar, and the United Arab Emirates). The British also had a great deal of influence in such Muslim countries as Persia (modern-day Iran) and Afghanistan.

Even in Muslim countries that were free of direct European influence,

Mustafa Kemal Atatürk (1881–1938) is considered the founder of modern Turkey. During his 15-year presidency he modeled Turkey's government on secular Western principles, rather than on Islamic law.

leaders incorporated Western ideas into their governments. A good example of this occurred in Turkey, where a secular state developed after the collapse of the Ottoman Empire.

The idea that religion and government should not be mixed is a characteristic of many Western political systems. Government is considered a public matter, while religion is a private one. Therefore, Western society is often divided into secular and sacred spheres—a concept called the "separation of church and state" in the United States. Traditionally, Muslim societies held a different idea—both political and religious authority could be vested in leaders, such as the caliphs who ruled the Islamic world after the death of the Prophet Muhammad. As the Ottoman empire rose to power, its sultans declared themselves the Muslim caliphs, and were therefore treated as religious leaders by Sunni Muslims living in the empire.

As the modern state of Turkey developed in the early 1920s, nationalist leaders like Mustafa Kemal Atatürk, the first president of Turkey, helped to adopt a Western-style legal system, wrote a constitution patterned after those in the West, and declared that the government would be based on secular principles rather than on Islamic law. In doing this, Turkey turned away from centuries of Islamic tradition and imitated the West.

Decisions made by the victorious powers after the First World War contributed to unrest in much of the Muslim world. For example, in India a nationalist movement gained widespread support after British troops massacred hundreds of protesters during the 1919 Punjab riots. The most influential leader for Indian independence was Mohandas K. Gandhi, a Hindu who advocated a policy of non-violent resistance to British rule. A less well-known, but no less important, Muslim leader was Muhammad Ali Jinnah, who also advocated for a separate Indian state. The efforts of Jinnah and other Muslim leaders would ultimately lead to the creation of a separate Muslim state, Pakistan, when India became independent in 1947.

Also, the example of European colonialism is believed by some scholars to have contributed to the outbreak of the Second World War. It can be argued that Japan's instigation of war in Asia and the Pacific Ocean during the late 1930s and early 1940s—during which the small country used force to seize a great deal of territory, just as the European colonial powers had in the previous century—shows Japan's success in adopting Western models of conquest.

In the decades that followed the end of World War II in 1945, the European empires began to shed their colonies and dependencies. There were at least two reasons for this. Some colonies, such as India, rebelled against their colonial status and demanded independence. Also, Great Britain, France, and other colonial powers were so depleted by the two world wars that they were unable to maintain their far-flung empires. However, the shift to independence would prove difficult. As former European colonies in Africa, the Middle East, the Caribbean, and Asia were fragmented into dozens of new independent states, they faced a multitude of social, economic, and political difficulties. Many countries emerged from colonial status only to become involved in serious internal disputes.

An example of this occurred in August 1947, when Great Britain granted independence to India. However, tensions between India's Hindu majority and its minority Muslim population led the British to divide the former colony into two states—India and Pakistan. This immediately led to violence between religious groups, during which an estimated 250,000 people were killed. A major refugee crisis also developed, during which Hindus and Sikhs fled Pakistan for India, while Muslims left India for Pakistan. It was estimated that more than 12 million people became refugees immediately after the 1947 partition.

Relations between India and Pakistan have never been good; a particular area of dispute has been the Kashmir province, which despite its majority Muslim population became part of India, rather than Pakistan, in 1947. The countries have gone to war over Kashmir three times (in 1947, 1965, and 1971). Tensions between India and Pakistan remain high, and the situation between the two countries has become even more dangerous because both countries now possess nuclear weapons.

After Pakistan became independent, it faced many other difficulties, including a geographic one—the country initially consisted of two sections that were almost a thousand miles apart. West Pakistan and East Pakistan could not work together, and after a 1971 civil war East Pakistan broke away and established itself as the independent country of Bangladesh.

In Pakistan, over the years elected governments have given way to military rule. Today, Pakistan is among the poorest countries in the world and is dangerously overpopulated. Economic development is hindered by the fact that the entire region regularly experiences destructive monsoons and floods. In its more than half a century of existence, Pakistan has been unable to solve its severe economic and social problems.

Text-Dependent Questions

1. What occurred at the 1884 Berlin West Africa Conference?
2. What is nationalism?

Research Project

Decisions made at the Paris Peace Conference of 1919, which was held after World War I, helped to reshape the modern world by creating new countries from the colonies or territories of the conquered powers (Germany, the Austro-Hungarian Empire, and the Ottoman Empire.) These new countries did not immediately gain independence; existing nations like France and Britain were given authority (known as a mandate) to rule them until they were ready for full independence. Using the Internet or your school library, find out more about the League of Nations and the mandate system, and write a two-page report on it. Was the mandate system a success, or a failure? Provide real-world examples to support your position.

6

US Involvement in the Middle East

Citizens of the United States generally see their country as a land of freedom and tolerance, with a responsibility to spread the ideals of liberty and democracy throughout the world. They point with pride to the US's role in doing this since its founding. During the 19th century, for example, the success of the American Revolution inspired independence movements throughout South and Central America; afterward, the United States discouraged European powers from retaking control of newly independent countries like Mexico, Colombia, and Haiti. In the 20th century, the US entered World War I to "make the world safe for democracy," and fought in World War II to stop German and Japanese aggression.

Americans are just as proud of their country's history after the Second World War. Through the Marshall Plan, the US provided economic aid to help rebuild Europe, and it also invested heavily in other developing countries. Since the late 1940s, the United States has pro-

Opposite: Iraqis in Baghdad protest against the city's occupation by US forces in April 2003. People in the Muslim world viewed the war against Iraq very differently from people in the United States. Many Muslims saw the US invasion as an aggressive move reminiscent of colonialism.

vided more humanitarian assistance each year than any other country. In 2014, for example, the US government provided approximately $6 billion in official humanitarian or development aid to other countries. This figure does not include billions more given as military aid or as government loans. In addition, according to an estimate by the US Agency for International Development (USAID), American citizens donate an additional $50 billion each year in non-official foreign aid.

In the decades after World War II the United States encouraged the breakup of the French and British colonial empires. More recently, the US government has used both force and diplomacy to resolve conflicts around the world. During the 1990s US troops fought in the Gulf War to liberate Kuwait, which had been invaded by its larger neighbor Iraq, and participated in peacekeeping missions in Somalia and Haiti, as well as in Bosnia and other states that were once part of Yugoslavia. During that decade US leaders tried to negotiate peaceful settlements to the Palestinian-Israeli conflict and the explosive situation in Northern Ireland. In March 2003, when the US and a coalition that included some of its allies attacked Iraq, the US government justified the operation by arguing that it would free the Iraqi people from the rule of an oppressive and brutal dictator.

The facts as seen from an American perspective tell only part of the story, however. People living outside the United States can point to numerous examples of US foreign policy during the second half of the 20th century that are just as manipulative and self-serving as the policies of any 19th-century imperial power. As a result, people in other parts of the world often do not view the United States's involvement in world affairs in the same positive light that US citizens do. Some see the US as a bully, looking only to protect its own interests. Others complain that the United

Words to Understand in This Chapter

ayatollah—highest rank of Shia Muslim religious leader.

ideology—a system of ideas and ideals, especially one that forms the basis of economic or political theory and policy.

States should do more to help the poor and oppressed people of the world.

Until the 1950s, the United States was widely admired in many Muslim countries. The European powers were disliked because they had suppressed nationalist and religious movements in their colonies in the Middle East and Central Asia. In countries like Iran, Turkey, and throughout the Arab world, the US was initially seen as a defender of independence that would protect them from invasion by the Union of Soviet Socialist Republics (USSR, or Soviet Union). However, attitudes began to change as the United States began to play a greater role in the affairs of Muslim countries.

The United States became involved in the Middle East during a period of world tensions known as the Cold War. From 1945 to 1991, the US and the Soviet Union—the world's two "superpowers"—each promoted their *ideology*: the communism of the Soviets versus the capitalism and democracy of the United States. In many ways, the foreign policies of both countries focused on limiting the other's influence.

The superpowers dominated the world politically and militarily during the Cold War. Both the US and the USSR used a variety of methods to compel countries around the world to join their side. These methods included military force, political corruption, and complex trade and military agreements. The United States became involved in wars in Korea and Vietnam in order to prevent the spread of communism in Asia, while the Soviets supported revolutionaries in Cuba and many countries of Central and South America.

During the Cold War the United States promoted itself as a champion of freedom and democracy, yet its foreign policy was often driven more by anti-communist goals than by pro-democratic ideals. Although many American allies, such as Great Britain and West Germany, had democratic forms of government, the United States also formed alliances with several unsavory dictators—in some cases, helping to overthrow democratically elected governments. During the 1950s and 1960s, the US supported—or helped to bring to power—repressive governments in such places as Chile, the Congo, South Vietnam, and Indonesia. In exchange the US-backed dictators in these countries opposed communism and the Soviet Union. This was the case in the Middle East as well. In countries like Iran and Pakistan,

Oil storage tanks at a refinery in Riyadh, Saudi Arabia. Because of the Western dependence on petroleum, the United States viewed oil-rich Middle Eastern countries like Saudi Arabia and Iran as important strategic partners, and supported repressive governments in these countries.

the US gave authoritarian governments financial and military aid because of their key strategic locations near the Soviet Union, and their willingness to oppose the spread of communism.

The large amount of oil in the Middle East—particularly in Arab countries like Saudi Arabia, Kuwait, and Iraq—was the main reason the region was strategically important during the Cold War. Petroleum is very important to the economies of industrialized nations like the United States, and countries in the Middle East control approximately 60 percent of the world's proven oil reserves. The US and other developed nations of the West wanted to make sure that the oil they needed would continue to flow, and could not be cut off by regimes that favored the Soviet Union. The US enlisted the ruling families of the oil-rich Arab states as allies in exchange for financial and military assistance. In 1951, for example, the United States signed a mutual defense agreement with Saudi Arabia. In 1957, President Dwight D. Eisenhower presented a new US policy, the "Eisenhower doctrine," which promised military and financial assistance to any country in the Middle East threatened by communism.

When the US government feared that oil-rich countries might leave its sphere of influence, it did not hesitate to become involved. An example of this occurred in Iran during the early 1950s. Iran (known as Persia until 1935) had been one of the first Middle Eastern countries in which oil was discovered. Foreign companies hurried to exploit this resource. In 1908, a British company, the Anglo-Persian Oil Company, was established; it soon became one of the most important oil companies in the world.

In 1926 a new shah, or ruler, came to power in Persia, Reza Shah Pahlavi. Over the next 15 years, he implemented many changes—reorganizing the country's legal and educational systems to be more like those found in Western nations, restricting the power of the Muslim clergy, and decreeing that Iranians should wear European-style clothing.

During World War II, Iran was invaded by the Soviet Union and Great Britain, who were allied in the fight against Nazi Germany. The shah, who favored Germany, was forced to abdicate the throne, and his son, Mohammad Reza Shah Pahlavi, became the country's new ruler. However, unrest in the country caused a new, reform-minded parliament to be elected, headed by a popular prime minister, Mohammed Mossadegh.

After the war ended, both Great Britain and the Soviet Union tried to negotiate new agreements to pump Iranian oil. Mossadegh and others wanted the country to produce and sell oil itself, rather than allowing outsiders to do so; this would bring even more money into Iran. Mossadegh proposed plans to nationalize Iran's oil industry.

In 1953, the US Central Intelligence Agency (CIA) supported a military coup that overthrew the Mossadegh government. This coup gave the shah more power over Iran's government. His rule was supported by US military and financial assistance over the next 25 years. During this time Iran gradually became even more Westernized. Those who objected to the shah's secular government or his program of reforms (called the White

When Iranian prime minister Mohammed Mossadegh (left) took steps to nationalize Iran's oil industry, the US Central Intelligence Agency supported a 1953 coup that overthrew his government and gave more power to the shah (right).

Revolution) were arrested or brutally suppressed. One opposition leader, the Shiite Muslim cleric *Ayatollah* Ruhollah Khomeini, was sent into exile in 1964. However, Khomeini continued to stir up opposition to the shah, arguing that his Western-influenced government was against the principles of Islam. Opposition to the shah's oppressive regime continued to grow during the 1970s, setting the stage for its overthrow in 1979.

The Cold War involvement of the United States and the Soviet Union in other countries often had long-lasting consequences—including anger and feelings of frustration among the people of countries in which the superpowers became involved. An example where involvement turned out badly for both the United States and the Soviet Union occurred in Afghanistan, a primarily Muslim country in Central Asia.

In December 1979 the Soviet Union invaded Afghanistan, overthrowing the government of Hafizullah Amin and establishing a puppet regime.

(Even though Amin had been a communist, the Soviets considered him unstable. A 1979 KGB report said that Amin was "insincere" toward the Soviet Union, and was pursuing "a more balanced foreign policy.")

Some religious Afghans fled to Pakistan and Iran, where they began to organize resistance to the communist regime, which did not permit Muslims to freely practice their religion. Muslim Afghans, who became known as *mujahideen*, soon began fighting to force the Soviets from their country. The *mujahideen* were not just Afghans; Muslims came from Saudi Arabia, Algeria, Egypt, China, the Philippines, and the Soviet republic of Chechnya to join the struggle against the USSR.

The CIA supported the *mujahideen*, providing an estimated $3 billion in weapons and military training. (One thing the *mujahideen* learned from the CIA was the concept of "strategic sabotage"—selecting targets that have a symbolic significance. Years later, a former member of the *mujahideen*, Osama bin Laden, would use this lesson with great effectiveness against the United States.)

US-supported *mujahideen* hold rockets near their base in the Safed Koh Mountains, 1988. The invasion of Afghanistan by the Soviet Union in 1979 resulted in a brutal ten-year conflict.

The *mujahideen's* fierce resistance prolonged the conflict over ten years, during which time approximately 15,000 Soviet soldiers were killed in combat and an estimated one million Afghan soldiers and civilians died. In 1989, the Soviets withdrew from Afghanistan without having achieved any significant political or military gains. Some political commentators and historians have argued that the lengthy and draining Soviet involvement in Afghanistan contributed greatly to the breakup of the Soviet Union in 1991, and therefore to the end of the Cold War.

However, having accomplished the goal in Afghanistan—to frustrate the Soviet Union and prevent the spread of communism—the United States also pulled out of the country after the Soviets left. Although the US had been willing to spend money on weapons and training, it was not willing to remain engaged and help build a stable government in Afghanistan after the Cold War ended. The resulting power vacuum meant that different groups of *mujahideen* fought for power in the country. By 1996, a group called the Taliban had established a religious government, based on a strict interpretation of Islamic principles, over most of Afghanistan. During its time in power, the Taliban was often criticized by the United Nations, the United States, and other countries for its record of human-rights abuses, particularly toward women. The regime was ultimately brought down by the United States in the fall of 2001.

"The Islamic fundamentalists would not [have come to] power in Afghanistan if not for US intervention," notes William Blum, author of *Killing Hope: US Military and CIA Interventions since World War II.* "The CIA orchestrated the symphony. They brought in warriors from over a dozen Muslim countries who were trained and armed."

While the US was involved in the Soviet-Afghan conflict, it was so focused on bringing down the Soviet Union that it ignored the fact that many of the militants recruited for the *mujahideen* had strong feelings against Western involvement in the Middle East. In Afghanistan, and in other parts of the Muslim world during the Cold War, people came to believe that US promises of equality and democracy were as empty as the promises of independence made by the European colonial powers during the early 20th century. People in the Muslim world were also uncomfortable with what they saw as the corrupting influence of Western culture on

Islamic society, and with the disparity between the wealth of the United States and other western nations and the poverty that was prevalent in Afghanistan, Pakistan, and other Muslim countries. Another issue that particularly angered Muslim fundamentalists was US support of Israel.

The US, Israel, and the Palestinians

The United States and Israel have enjoyed a long, close relationship. In May 1948, when Jewish leaders in Palestine declared the independent state of Israel, the United States was the first country to officially recognize its government. Today, Israel is the largest recipient of US foreign aid, receiving approximately $3 billion each year in military and economic assistance. The United States has worked to help Israel become accepted by the world community, while in the United Nations Israel has voted in agreement with the United States more often than any other country.

During the first two decades of the Jewish state's existence, the relationship between the US and Israel was not as close as it is today. The US government provided a small amount of financial aid but no military assistance, and did not permit sales of US weapons or military technology to Israel. In 1956, when Israel occupied Egyptian territory, the US intervened in favor of the Arab state and forced Israel to withdraw.

This crisis developed when Egypt's president, Gamal Abdel Nasser, announced plans for the government to take over the Suez Canal. This waterway, which connects the Mediterranean Sea to the Indian Ocean via the Red Sea, was a key route for world trade—particularly for oil shipments from the Persian Gulf. It had been built by British and French companies, which controlled the canal until it was nationalized. Nasser also blockaded the Straits of Tiran, Israel's only outlet into the Red Sea.

In response, British, French, and Israeli leaders secretly made plans to seize the canal and overthrow Nasser's government. Israel invaded Egypt, attacking targets on the Sinai Peninsula from which it could control one side of the canal. The British and French, on the pretext of protecting their shipping, sent troops in to capture the other side of the canal. However, the United States publicly opposed this plan, even though France and Britain were considered close allies. Pressure by President

Eisenhower forced the invaders to pull out of Egypt and leave Nasser in control of the canal.

The fact that the US had supported an Arab country over its major European allies was greatly appreciated by Muslims in the Middle East. However, Arab and Muslim attitudes toward the United States changed as the US-Israel relationship warmed during the 1960s. This was particularly true after Israel defeated the armies of Egypt, Syria, and Jordan in the June 1967 War (also known as the Six-Day War). Israel, believing the Arab countries were preparing to attack, launched a preemptive strike on June 5, 1967, which destroyed the Egyptian air force. By the time the fighting ended on June 10, Israeli troops had captured East Jerusalem and the West Bank from Jordan, the Gaza Strip and Sinai Peninsula from Egypt, and the Golan Heights from Syria. This territory more than doubled the size of Israel.

One reason US policy toward Israel changed from the 1950s to the 1960s was because of shifts in the Cold War. During the Suez crisis, one of the reasons Eisenhower pressured Britain, France, and Israel to withdraw was because he did not want the Soviet Union to become involved in the crisis. The USSR had been trying to build closer ties with Egypt and other Arab countries, and Eisenhower hoped siding with Nasser would reduce Soviet influence in the Middle East. The Eisenhower doctrine, formulated in 1957, provided a basis for the US to oppose the spread of communism in the region. By the 1960s, however, the Soviet Union was openly selling arms to Egypt and other Arab countries. The US saw a strong Israel as a bulwark against the spread of communism into the Middle East, and wanted to make sure the country remained stronger than its neighbors. Israel used mostly French weapons to fight the June 1967 War, but after the Israeli victory the US became Israel's main supplier of military hardware and economic assistance.

However, the Israeli occupation of territories captured in the June 1967 War—particularly the capture of East Jerusalem, where several important Islamic shrines are located—deeply offended Muslims around the world. After 1967 Israel promised that it would give up the territories in exchange for peace agreements with its Arab neighbors. However, peace did not seem likely after leaders of the Arab states met in Khartoum

An Israeli police officer arrests a Palestinian demonstrator at the Damascus Gate of East Jerusalem, 2013. Control over East Jerusalem, which was captured by Israeli forces during the June 1967 War, has been an important issue in Israeli-Palestinian negotiations.

and adopted the "three no" policy: no peace with Israel, no recognition of Israel, and no negotiations with Israel.

Although the Arabs rejected Israel's "land for peace" offer, when Israelis began to build settlements in the occupied territories many Muslims became even angrier. Some orthodox Jews defended the right of Israelis to settle in this land, claiming a divine right—according to the Torah, God had told the Jews to settle throughout the "promised land." Opponents of the settlements protested that they violated international law and would ultimately lead to Israeli annexation of the occupied territories. Another issue was the ownership of land on which settlements were built. Although much of the land had been uninhabited, some settlements were built on land once owned by Palestinian Arabs, who had fled the region during the various wars.

Before and during Israel's 1948–49 war for independence, between

500,000 and 750,000 Palestinians had left their homes. Some moved to the West Bank or Gaza Strip, which during the war were seized by Jordan and Egypt. Other Palestinians ended up in hastily built refugee camps in Lebanon, Syria, or Jordan. The June 1967 War led another wave of Palestinians to leave their homes in Israel and flee to the refugee camps. At the same time, the Israeli capture and occupation of the West Bank and Gaza Strip placed more than a million Palestinian Arabs under the control of Israel's government. Israeli troops enforced martial law throughout the occupied territories, and Palestinians had few rights in Israeli society. The Israeli government also assumed title to property left behind by Palestinian refugees and distributed that property to settlers.

After the June 1967 War, Palestinian opposition to Israel became more radical. Groups like the Palestine Liberation Organization (PLO) soon began carrying out terrorist attacks against Israeli targets. Israel retaliated by bombing PLO bases in Lebanon and Jordan and assassinating suspected Palestinian leaders. In 1982, Israel invaded southern Lebanon, with the support of the United States, to drive out the PLO. Although most Israeli troops were withdrawn by 1985, Israel continued to occupy a "buffer zone" in southern Lebanon until May 2000.

Since the June 1967 War, the United States government has tried to

Israeli immigrants settle at Tarshiha, in the Galilee, in houses abandoned by Palestinian Arabs who fled the country during the unrest of 1947–49. It is estimated that at least a half million Palestinians fled their homes before and during Israel's war for independence. Hundreds of thousands more Palestinians became refugees during the June 1967 War.

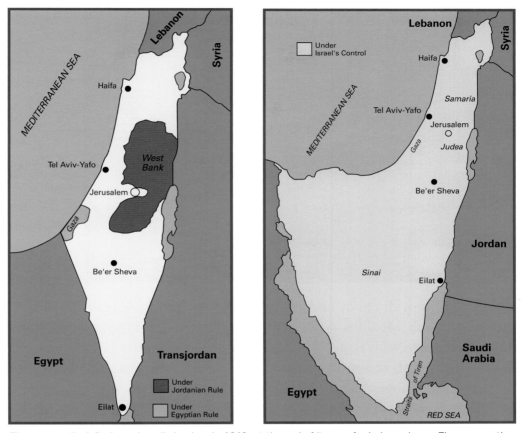

The map on the left shows Israel's borders in 1949, at the end of its war for Independence. The map on the right shows the territory under Israeli control
at the end of the June 1967 War.

facilitate efforts toward peace in the Middle East. After Egypt and Syria attacked Israel in October 1973, US Secretary of State Henry Kissinger held numerous meetings with leaders of the three countries in order to arrange a cease-fire. Kissinger's "shuttle diplomacy" led to a thawing of relations between the US and Egypt, and would provide an opening for a historic Middle East peace treaty.

In September 1978, US President Jimmy Carter negotiated a peace agreement between Israeli prime minister Menachem Begin and Egyptian president Anwar Sadat at a summit held at the presidential retreat at Camp David. The Camp David Accords, as the agreement between these long-time enemies became known, were seen as a positive development by

Jimmy Carter (center) listens as Menachem Begin (left) expresses a point to Anwar Sadat during their 1978 meeting at Camp David. During the historic summit, the leaders hammered out a peace agreement between Egypt and Israel.

most of the world. Sadat and Begin shared the 1978 Nobel Peace Prize. However, Arab Muslims were angry that Egypt, the largest Arab state, had made peace with Israel. Egypt was expelled from the League of Arab States, most Arab countries broke off diplomatic relations, and a Muslim extremist assassinated Sadat in 1981.

The Camp David Accords actually consisted of two agreements. In the first, Egypt promised peace and Israel agreed to return the Sinai Peninsula it had held since 1967. This treaty has remained in effect since it was signed in 1979, and Israel fulfilled its obligation by withdrawing from the Sinai in stages. The second agreement was a framework for negotiations to eventually create an autonomous state in the West Bank and Gaza Strip. This section of the treaty was vaguely worded, however, and no progress was made toward establishing a Palestinian state.

Angered by continued delays, and frustrated by poverty and oppressive living conditions, in 1987 a series of protests against the Israeli occupation began in Gaza and the West Bank. This uprising became known as the *intifada*. Israeli troops responded to stone-throwing demonstrations by angry Palestinian civilians with force. According to B'Tselem, an Israeli human-rights group, more than 1,100 Palestinians and about 100 Israeli civilians were killed between 1987 and 1993.

In 1993, after secret negotiations in Oslo, Norway, Israel agreed to gradually permit limited Palestinian self-government in the occupied territories, and to continue negotiations aimed at further satisfying the concerns of both parties. In September 1993, an agreement known as the Declaration of Principles was signed on the White House lawn, and sealed with a handshake between Israeli prime minister Yitzhak Rabin and PLO leader Yasir Arafat.

Over the next few years some progress was made toward a permanent solution to the Israeli-Palestinian problem. A provisional government, the Palestinian Authority, was formed in 1994, and the next year Israel gave the authority control over parts of the West Bank. However, extremists on both sides made a fair peace settlement difficult. In Israel, orthodox Jews were angry at the country's surrender of territory; an Israeli militant assassinated Rabin in November 1995. After Benjamin Netanyahu, an opponent of the peace process, was elected prime minister in May 1996, he angered Muslims by authorizing an archaeological dig under the al-Aqsa mosque, one of the holiest Islamic sites. On the Palestinian side, Arafat's efforts to maintain order were undercut by a devastating campaign of suicide bombings against both the Israeli military and civilians. The attacks, by the militant organization Hamas, further poisoned the prospects for peace.

US President Bill Clinton pressured both Israelis and Palestinians to

The signing of the 1993 Declaration of Principles appeared to set a course for eventual Palestinian statehood and peace with Israel. The historic handshake on the White House lawn between Israeli prime minister Yitzhak Rabin and PLO leader Yasir Arafat was praised in the West. However, the path to peace during the 1990s was rocky, and the process ultimately failed after a July 2000 summit sponsored by US president Bill Clinton at Camp David.

keep moving forward with the peace process, despite accusations by both sides that the other was not complying with the 1993 Declaration of Principles. In 1998 Israel turned over control of more territory to the Palestinian Authority. However, in 1999 a five-year deadline for Palestinian statehood, which had been set in the original Oslo Accords, passed without the two sides agreeing on the most important issues—the borders of the Palestinian state, the status of East Jerusalem, and the right of refugees to return to their homes in Israel. Arafat threatened to declare statehood unilaterally, but Clinton persuaded him to wait until an agreement could be reached with Israel. In July 2000 Clinton hosted a summit at Camp David between Arafat and Israeli prime minister Ehud Barak, who had been elected on a promise to create a lasting peace with the Palestinians. The talks failed.

The Palestinians were tired of waiting. In September of that year a second Palestinian *intifada* began in the occupied territories, as Palestinians began a campaign of suicide bombing attacks. Israel responded by replacing Palestinian self-rule with martial law, restricting Palestinian freedoms, and retaliating against suicide attacks with military force. The prospect for peace vanished beneath new waves of terror and repression.

In the West, Yasir Arafat received most of the blame for the collapse of the peace process. News reports painted Arafat as stubborn and not committed to peace, saying that Barak had offered "99 percent" of what the Palestinians had been asking for. Clinton himself said that Arafat was the reason the summit had failed. Arafat was also blamed for not doing enough to stop the violence of the second *intifada*.

People in the Muslim world saw the failure of the peace process differently. They felt that Clinton, who was supposed to be an impartial facilitator to the peace process during the 1990s, had instead sided with the Israelis, giving in to their demands while trying to wring additional concessions from Arafat. From the Palestinian point of view, Barak's proposal at Camp David did not fairly address the most important issues, such as the right of Palestinian refugees to return to their homes in Israel or receive compensation for their property. Also, the territory that Israel was prepared to concede was less than Palestinians felt they had been promised in the past. In the end, Arafat and the Palestinians felt that they had been betrayed both by Israel, which had not lived up to its promises, and by the United States, which had not forced Israel to meet its commitments.

Palestinians cited the continued growth of settlements in the occupied territories as a sign that Israel had not acted in good faith during the peace process. In 1990, there had been approximately 76,000 Israeli settlers in some 150 settlements. By 2000, the population of Israeli settlements had increased to more than 200,000. Although Clinton called the settlements "obstacles to peace," he never used his leverage with the Israelis to stop their construction and expansion.

The Israeli-Palestinian conflict remains a critical issue in disagreements between Muslims and the West. In 2005, Israel dismantled all 21 settlements in the Gaza Strip, along with four in the West Bank. However, it has continued to both expand other settlements and settle new areas in the West Bank, East Jerusalem, and the Golan Heights, despite international condemnation. Arabs—and many other Muslims—feel that the US supports Israel at the expense of the Palestinians, and consider Israel a puppet of the United States.

Revolution in Iran

During 1979, people living in the United States were shocked to see television images of angry crowds in Iran burning American flags and shouting anti-US slogans. In November 1979, a group of students attacked the American embassy in Tehran, capturing more than 50 people and holding them hostage for 444 days.

The Iranian revolution, in which the shah's US-supported regime was overthrown by a popular nationwide movement and replaced with an Islamic-based theocracy, surprised people in the United States. Westerners were also upset at the depth of anti-American feeling voiced during and after the Iranian revolution.

By the late 1970s, many Iranians were unhappy with the shah's oppressive government, its embrace of Westernization, and its heavy spending. In 1978 a series of labor strikes and national protests crippled the economy, and Ayatollah Khomeini, who was still living in exile, insist-

Demonstrators in Tehran lift a shrouded body over the heads of a crowd during a 1978 protest. In Iran, anger against the shah's repressive government finally led to a series of national strikes and protests; when people were killed in violent clashes with the shah's police, they were mourned by huge, riotous crowds. As the country ground to a standstill, the shah left Iran in January 1979 to undergo a medical procedure in the United States. The next month, exiled Iranian Shiite cleric Ayatollah Ruhollah Khomeini returned to Iran. The shah's government was overthrown and a theocracy, headed by Khomeini, was instituted.

ed that the shah relinquish power. In January 1979, with his control over the government crumbling, the shah left Iran for a medical procedure. He would never return. The next month, Khomeini returned to Iran and took control. Soon, Khomeini and his followers had established a conservative government in Iran strictly based on Shiite Islamic principles.

Under the shah, Iran had been a key US ally in the Middle East. However, Khomeini viewed the United States as the greatest enemy of Islam, often referring to the US as the "Great Satan." (Iran did not side with the USSR in the Cold War, however, as Khomeini hated the Soviet Union nearly as much as he hated the US) The Iranians broke diplomatic relations with the United States and began trying to eliminate Western influences from Iranian society.

In the more than 30 years since the Iranian Revolution, relations between the United States and Iran have remained hostile and combative. In his January 2002 State of the Union address, President George W. Bush called Iran part of an "axis of evil," along with Iraq and North Korea. For more than a decade, Western nations backed by the United Nations Security Council imposed economic sanctions on Iran due to concerns that the country was trying to develop nuclear weapons. Finally, in 2015, Iran agreed to shelf its nuclear program in exchange for the sanctions being lifted.

Unrest in the Persian Gulf

From the time it was conceived, Iran's theocratic government worried its neighbors. Khomeini angered the leaders of other Persian Gulf countries when he declared that his revolution should be extended to overthrow these countries' governments. As a result, the United States sent military technology to Saudi Arabia to defend that kingdom from a possible attack. The US also grew closer with the ruling families of other Gulf states, such as Qatar, the United Arab Emirates, Oman, and Bahrain. The US did not want to see Khomeini's Islamic revolution spread from Iran into the other Gulf states, so it provided funds to help support the monarchies in these Arab countries.

In September 1980, Iraq, a Gulf Arab state, went to war against Iran. Iraq's ruler, Saddam Hussein, felt that his secular government was threatened by Khomeini's religious-based rule; he also thought that his smaller country could seize Iranian territory while that larger country was in turmoil. Although the United States proclaimed its neutrality, it did become indirectly involved as the conflict dragged out over eight years, providing weapons and other support to Iraq.

Once again, however, the United States was supporting a dictator, Saddam Hussein, who had not only started the Iran-Iraq War, but also used chemical weapons to kill thousands of Iranian soldiers during the war. Saddam even used these deadly weapons on his own citizens—Kurdish Iraqis—in order to strengthen his hold on power.

During the Iran-Iraq War, Saddam Hussein's government borrowed heavily from Saudi Arabia, the Soviet Union, Kuwait, and other countries to finance the war. After the war ended, Saddam needed money to pay his debts. Because Iraq has the world's second-largest proven reserve of oil (after Saudi Arabia), Saddam wanted to sell more oil; this would provide the additional money he needed to repay his creditors.

Iraq is a member of the Organization of Petroleum Exporting Countries (OPEC), an eleven-nation cartel that tries to set world oil prices by controlling the amount of oil on the market. OPEC does this by establishing production quotas for each of its members, in order to regulate the amount of oil that is available. However, in the 1980s an increase in oil from non-OPEC sources in Mexico and the North Sea, and a worldwide economic depression that reduced the need for petroleum, led to a glut in the oil market that caused prices to fall. As a result, the other OPEC countries wanted to restrict, rather than loosen, production quotas. OPEC refused Iraq's request to increase its oil production.

Saddam Hussein also asked the Saudi and Kuwaiti governments to forgive his debts. The billions they had given to Iraq should be considered grants, rather than loans, he argued, because Iraq was protecting the rest of the Gulf states from Iranian domination and the spread of the Islamic revolution. The Saudis and Kuwaitis rejected this request.

With Iraq facing a major economic crisis, Saddam decided on a third course of action—an invasion of Kuwait. Annexing Kuwait and its oil fields would give Iraq control over more than 20 percent of the world's oil, and would enable him to quickly raise more money to resolve Iraq's economic problems.

Kuwait had a history as an independent sheikhdom dating back to the mid-18th century, while Iraq had only been established as an independent country in 1932. (The boundaries of Iraq were established by the League of Nations after World War I.) However, over the years various Iraqi rulers had claimed that Iraq should control Kuwait because the Ottomans had once governed both territories together. Kuwait, and the rest of the world, had always rejected this claim. In August 1990 Iraq invaded Kuwait and Saddam Hussein declared it the 19th province of Iraq.

The annexation of Kuwait was more than just a seizure of oil fields; it was an attempt by Saddam Hussein to shift the balance of power in the Middle East clearly in Iraq's favor. Saddam wanted to be the dominant power in the Middle East, and also wanted to increase his global stature by being able to control the price of oil on world markets. He believed that the world would be upset about the invasion, but would ultimately lack the resolve to do anything about it. If he had been successful in annexing Kuwait, he would have become a major player in the world scene.

As Iraqi troops moved across Kuwait toward Saudi Arabia, the ruling Al Saud family feared that their country might be the next to fall to Saddam's armies. Saudi King Fahd asked the United States for assistance, which the US was quick to provide. Its intelligence indicated that Iraqi troops could roll over Saudi Arabia as quickly as they had conquered Kuwait. If Iraq could pacify and rule Saudi Arabia, Saddam Hussein would control more than 40 percent of the world's oil. US troops were quickly flown to defensive positions in the Arabian desert—Operation

US Army Abrams battle tanks move across the desert of northern Kuwait during Operation Desert Storm.

Desert Shield. At the same time, the United Nations Security Council issued a resolution condemning the Iraqi takeover of Kuwait.

Over the next few months, as Saddam defied U.N. demands that he withdraw from Kuwait, and as stories came out about looting, destruction, and atrocities committed against Kuwaiti citizens, the international community came together in opposition to Iraq's aggression. The United States joined with more than 30 other countries—including many Muslim nations—to form a military coalition. Saddam Hussein was given a deadline of January 15, 1991, to pull his forces out of Iraq. When the deadline passed with no change in the situation, coalition forces attacked, starting the 1991 Gulf War.

The war was over quickly. After a period of aerial bombardment and missile attacks against military and industrial targets, coalition ground forces invaded Iraq in February 1991. Within a week they had routed the Iraqi army and forced it out of Kuwait. By the time the US imposed a cease-fire to end the slaughter, between 100,000 and 150,000 Iraqi soldiers had been killed, wounded, or captured. By contrast, the coalition forces lost only 370 combatants.

When the war ended, Iraq was plunged into turmoil as minority groups—Kurds in the north and Shiite Muslims in the south—rebelled against Saddam Hussein's government. The rebellious Shiites and Kurds had expected the United States to provide help, in the hope that their uprisings would ultimately topple Saddam from power. However, the US did not intervene initially, allowing the Iraqi army to put down the rebellions swiftly and brutally.

The U.N. Security Council passed resolutions setting the conditions for ending the war—Iraq was to renounce its claim to Kuwait and destroy all its weapons of mass destruction. The US would maintain economic sanctions against the country until Iraq complied. The embargo made life extremely difficult for most Iraqis. It became hard for people to find food and medicine. However, the sanctions had only limited success. As dictator of Iraq, Saddam Hussein had a great amount of control over the country's economy. He continued to become richer, building a personal fortune valued at more than $7 billion, while many of his people faced starvation, medical problems, and shortages of essential items.

To alleviate the suffering of Iraq's people, in the mid-1990s the United Nations started a program that permitted Iraq to sell its oil in exchange for food, medicine, and other goods necessary for its citizens. Some people criticized the "oil-for-food" program, saying the money brought in by Iraq's sale of oil helped Saddam's regime remain in power, instead of helping ordinary Iraqis. Others criticized the U.N. sanctions, seeing them as the cause of much suffering among the Iraqi people. However, defenders of the "oil for food" program noted that the economic sanctions did not prohibit food, medicine, or humanitarian aid. They also pointed out that Saddam had not even agreed to participate in the program for more than 18 months after it was initially proposed by the United Nations, and that he had not used the money to alleviate his people's suffering.

People in the Arab Muslim world were particularly resentful about the continued sanctions and their effect on the ordinary people of Iraq. They also denounced what they saw as Western imperialism in the region, as US and British fighter jets patrolled "no-fly zones" over the northern and southern parts of Iraq. These zones were justified as protection for Iraq's Kurdish and Shiite populations, which had been oppressed by Saddam Hussein in the past. However, US attacks on targets within Iraq between 1991 and 2001, and the US-led invasion and occupation of the country in 2003, fueled the anger of many Muslims toward the United States and its continued involvement in the Middle East.

Text-Dependent Questions

1. What were the Camp David Accords?
2. When did the second *intifada* begin?

Research Project

Using the Internet or your school library, learn more about the world leaders who were involved in the decision to go to war against Iraq in 1991, such as George H.W. Bush, Margaret Thatcher, Mikhail Gorbachev, Hosni Mubarak, or King Fahd. Write a two-page report about this leader's political career and accomplishments. Share your report with the class.

7

Islam and the West Today

T he collapse of communist states in Eastern Europe beginning in 1989 and the breakup of the Soviet Union in 1991 marked the end of the Cold War. Many of the new countries that emerged from the former USSR—countries like Azerbaijan, Kazakhstan, Kyrgyzstan, Tajikistan, Turkmenistan, and Uzbekistan— have large Muslim populations. These states are struggling to establish political, economic, and social stability.

Azerbaijan, for example, was once a Soviet republic. Since its independence in 1991, it has been involved in a border dispute with Armenia, another former Soviet republic that has a large Christian population. As a result of this conflict, Azerbaijan has lost control of nearly a fifth of its territory and some 750,000 Muslims have become homeless refugees. Even though Azerbaijan's government controls substantial oil deposits it has been unable to use its money to improve living conditions for most of its people. One reason for this is wide-

Opposite: United Nations forensic experts unearth victims from a mass grave near Srebrenica, Bosnia and Herzegovina. Violence in the Balkans during the 1990s often pitted Christians against Muslims. In July 1995 Bosnian Serbs massacred nearly 8,000 Muslim men and boys at Srebrenica.

spread corruption among businesspeople and government officials.

Bosnia and Herzegovina is another country that has had difficulties since the early 1990s. After declaring its independence from Yugoslavia in 1991, the country has been torn by bitter internal conflicts between ethnic groups. Until 1995, Serbs—the dominant ethnic group in Bosnia—conducted a campaign of "ethnic cleansing" against Muslims and non-Serbians. In 1995 the North Atlantic Treaty Organization (NATO) intervened and ended the war. Since then, the country has slowly been establishing a free market economy. The region's large black market, however, seriously undermines the government's economic policies. Accordingly, the bulk of the population is still very poor.

Independence was supposed to revitalize Azerbaijan, Bosnia and Herzegovina, and dozens of other nations in the post–Cold War world. The reality, however, is that social and economic development are difficult processes that cannot be accomplished in just a few years. Attempts to rapidly change these developing nations have created social turmoil, and efforts to blend Islamic beliefs with Western ideology have met with mixed results.

During the Cold War, as the United States became entangled in the Muslim world, more and more Muslims took a skeptical view of the reasons behind US and Western involvement in their countries. Many Muslims began to see themselves as a distinct cultural group whose interests differed sharply from those of the West. As the Cold War wore on, Islamists began to speak in opposition to the West. At first their voices were low, but by the late 1970s they were making themselves heard loudly, and sometimes violently.

What Is Islamism?

The word *fundamentalism* was invented in the early twentieth century to describe conservative Christian beliefs (particularly, an emphasis on literal interpretation of the Bible as fundamental to Christian life and teaching). Today the word is commonly used to refer to any religious movement that preaches a return to basic or traditional beliefs. News reports sometimes refer to "Muslim fundamentalists" when referring to people who wish to use a strict interpretation of Islamic law (Sharia) as the basis for their government and society. Contemporary scholars prefer to use the term *Islamism* rather than "fundamentalism" to describe this ideology.

Islamists believe that they must base their lives on Qur'anic principles. Some take a moderate view, arguing that the Qur'an must be interpreted in light of contemporary conditions. Others are more extreme, and are willing to use violence in order to spread their interpretation of the Qur'an. Whether extreme or moderate, however, Islamists are politically active people who are willing to use modern technology and methods in the service of Islam. There are two issues central to Islamism. One is a commitment to help the poorer members of Muslim society, the other is a rejection of certain aspects of Western culture.

The Qur'an tells Muslims that they are responsible for helping the poor and needy in their communities. Islamists today take this responsibility very seriously. They see a wide disparity between rich and poor in Muslim countries like Saudi Arabia and Kuwait. In other countries with large Muslim populations, like India, Pakistan, and Afghanistan, poverty is widespread. And in general, people in the Muslim world are significantly less wealthy than people in the United States and the West. According to 2014 figures from the World Bank, the average annual income in the United States is $54,629, compared to $1,875 in Sudan, $1,316 in Pakistan, and $633 in Afghanistan. Islamists criticize wealthy members of their own societies for not doing enough to help the poor. They have been critical of the West for the same reason.

In addition, Islamists feel that their own cultures are being lost or corrupted by Western influences. They believe that Western economic policies are unfair to Muslims, and that Western movies and television shows spread ideals that corrode Muslim values and morals, by glamorizing drug and alcohol use, sexual promiscuity, and materialism.

Islamists therefore reject those elements of Western culture that they feel violate their religious principles. Islamists see themselves as trying to incorporate and harmonize Islamic values with the modern world, but they feel that they must take action to reduce or eliminate Western influences in their societies. The Islamist view of jihad requires Muslims to defend themselves against cultural and social corruption.

Islamism and Government

Throughout the Muslim world there has been a disagreement in recent decades about the amount of influence Islam—particularly a conservative Islamist version of the religion—should have in government. An example of this can be seen in Egypt, which had been ruled by an authoritarian president, Hosni Mubarak, since 1981. In 2010, a wave of uprisings and protests for democracy, known as the "Arab Spring," began in Tunisia and soon spread to other Arab countries. Mubarak was deposed by an Egyptian uprising in the spring of 2011. When democratic elections were held, Mohamed Morsi, a leader of the Islamist organization Muslim Brotherhood, was elected president. However, the Muslim Brotherhood and the military soon clashed over control of the country. Morsi oversaw the drafting of a new constitution in 2012, but he was criticized for trying to expand his powers as president. Some Egyptians became disillusioned since his government did not seem to be as democratic as they had hoped. By June 2013, many Egyptians were demonstrating in the streets again, this time calling for Morsi to be removed from office. The military removed Morsi the following month in a coup d'état led by General Abdel Fattah el-Sisi. In May 2014, Egyptians voted for a new constitution and elected el-Sisi to be their president.

There are many Islamist organizations and groups, and these differ ideologically in very significant and essential ways. For example, the contemporary Muslim Brotherhood organizations in Egypt and Jordan have renounced violence, and have successfully participated in the electoral and parliamentary processes in their respective countries. Islamist parties have peacefully co-existed with governments in places like Malaysia, Qatar, and Kuwait, and have often formed an important part of civil society. In Turkey, the Justice and Progress Party (AKP), described as a moderate party with Islamist roots, has held power since November 2002.

When secular governments try to stop popular Islamist movements, violence often results. In Algeria, after a single party had controlled the country's secular government for 30 years, a group called the Islamic Salvation Front (FIS) won provincial elections in the early 1990s that gave it a majority in the national assembly. The success of FIS at the ballot box led to the intervention of the Algerian military, which resulted in a vicious civil war in Algeria. Because the Islamist government had been unfairly preempted, some Islamists resorted to violence. A militant wing of the FIS, the Armed Islamic Group (GIA) drew international criticism for its terrorist activities, which included the slaughter of thousands of Algerian moderates. The FIS ultimately renounced violence and officially disbanded its paramilitary wing in 2000, but the GIA continued operating, although on a much smaller scale.

Other Islamist organizations have combined social activism and political activity with terrorist activities. Hezbollah ("Party of God") is a Lebanese group of Shiite militants that was formed to oppose Israel's 1982 occupation of southern Lebanon. The organization has grown into a political force in Lebanon, where it controls a bloc of seats in the country's parliament. One of Hezbollah's goals is to create a fundamentalist state, modeled on Iran, in Lebanon. Hezbollah has gained support from

Islamism and Terrorism

Militant Islamist groups often interpret the concept of jihad to justify acts of violence. Because these groups are often small, with limited resources, they have found terrorism to be their most effective weapon.

Terrorism can be defined as violence carried out for political purposes. For centuries it has been used as a political tool, and as a way for people who feel oppressed to fight back against their oppressors. Many groups and organizations have used terrorism to try to achieve their goals—anarchists in Russia, nationalists in Northern Ireland, fascists in Germany and Italy, separatists in Spain, leftist rebels in Colombia and Peru, socialists in Latin America and Europe, and white supremacists in the United States. Today people living in Israel are often victims of terrorism, but before Israel's war for independence Jewish extremists carried out terrorist attacks against British targets, such as the 1946 bombing of the King David Hotel in Jerusalem. Such attacks were intended to drive out the British and lead to the establishment of an independent Jewish state in Palestine.

In the present day many people living in the United States equate the word "terrorist" with "Muslim." This is an unfair stereotype. The majority of the world's Muslims condemn terrorism, and most mainstream Islamic scholars and teachers point out that suicide bombings and other acts of terrorism have no place in Islam—that Islam is a religion of peace. The governments of many Muslim countries condemn terrorist attacks, and have cooperated with the United States in the "war on terrorism."

Shiite Muslims in southern Lebanon because it established a network of schools, mosques, and medical clinics, and provided charitable assistance to people in need.

The dark side to this organization is that Hezbollah has regularly used violence against Western or Israeli targets as a way to achieve its political goals. During the 1980s, it kidnapped or assassinated dozens of Westerners in Lebanon. Hezbollah agents carried out the 1983 bombing of a US Marine barracks in Beirut that killed 241 American marines. Hezbollah has attacked Israeli targets both in southern Lebanon and within Israel, as well as Jewish targets elsewhere. Hezbollah also fought against Israel during the 2006 Lebanon War.

The militant Palestinian organization Hamas is another group that has used terrorism to further its political agenda. Like Hezbollah, Hamas has established a network that provides social services to many Palestinians within the occupied Gaza Strip territory and in the Palestinian refugee camps located in Jordan and other neighboring Arab states. However, the organization is dedicated to establishing an Islamist government in the region and to the destruction of Israel. Hamas plans and carries out suicide bombing attacks against both military and civilian targets inside Israel. These attacks have killed hundreds of Israelis, leading to violent reprisals by the Israeli military against the Palestinians; they contributed greatly to the collapse of the Arab-Israeli peace process.

In recent years, as Islamists have gained control of some countries or territories, there has been an increase in violence. The year 2013 saw the rise of the Islamic State of Iraq and the Levant (ISIL), which was able to capture and hold territory in both Iraq and Syria. By June 2014, after conquering the city of Mosul in Iraq, ISIL declared itself to be the restoration of the Islamic caliphate. ISIL's extremist leaders claimed that all Muslims needed to swear allegiance to their organization and follow its dictates, and that Islam needed to be returned to a "pure" state by eliminating apostates, or those who do not follow their teachings. ISIL attempted to do this in the territories it controlled by murdering Christians, Jews, Kurds, Shiite Muslims, Druze, and others living in the regions it controlled. The reports of ISIL atrocities led the United States, Russia, Turkey, France and other countries to intervene in the Syrian civil

People pay tribute at the Place de la Republique to the victims of the November 2015 terrorist attacks in Paris.

war with military force. Airstrikes were launched against ISIL positions and the US and other countries provided support to anti-ISIL factions fighting in Syria.

As Western nations have opposed the spread of ISIL, that organization has encouraged radical Muslims to attack Western targets. For example, in November 2015 Muslim extremists carried out mass shootings and suicide bombings in Paris that killed 137 people and wounded 368. Other notable terrorist attacks conducted by extremists in the name of Islam include the Boston Marathon bombing in 2013; the attack on the US embassy in Benghazi, Libya, in 2012; the Fort Hood shooting in 2009, in which a Muslim military officer killed 13 American soldiers; and the September 11 al-Qaeda attacks on the World Trade Center and the Pentagon in 2001.

Most Muslims condemn the terrorist activities of groups like Hezbollah and al-Qaeda, or the atrocities committed by ISIL. However, the numerous terrorist events involving Muslims over the past 45 years have created a stereotype of the "Islamic terrorist" targeting Westerners.

Terrorism is a world issue, not one that concerns only Westerners or Muslims. Even though groups like al-Qaeda have the ability to terrorize on a large scale, the reason they resort to terrorism is because they have little real power. Terrorists look at the rich and powerful West and they are overwhelmed. They are afraid that those who actually hold power will never address their concerns unless the terrorists can get their attention.

Conclusion: the Future

The cultural differences between Muslims and the countries of the West are real and significant. Still, the things that bind Muslims and Westerners together as humans are far greater than the things that divide them culturally. All humans want to live without fear. All humans want their basic needs to be satisfied. All humans want to be at peace with themselves, their families, and their communities.

When speaking of the Islamic world, or the Western world, it is important to keep in mind that within each of these general "worlds" there are great differences. France and the United States have vastly different histories, languages, and cultures, yet they are both considered Western nations. Likewise, Indonesia and Iran have vastly different histories, languages, and cultures, yet both are Islamic countries. It is impossible to discuss the Western or the Islamic world without overlooking important variations within individual countries. Nevertheless, in general the countries of the Western and Islamic worlds do hold fundamental ideas in common.

Although there are significant differences between Islamic and Western cultures, this does not mean that Muslims and Westerners cannot coexist peacefully. It does mean that Muslims and Westerners will have to work together to understand and accept each other. The Western process of understanding the Muslim world needs to begin with a commitment to stop regarding Muslim countries as backwards. Many Muslim countries are struggling to incorporate the modern technology of the West without betraying the Islamic heritage of their people.

Westerners need to understand the enormity of the task that these countries are undertaking and respond with patience and respect.

Some problems that Westerners and Muslims can solve together are the political, economic, and social circumstances that hinder Muslim development. These were created by the Western practice of exploiting their colonies rather than developing them. Westerners must work with Muslims to help them solve their problems—they cannot solve problems for them, and should not tell them how to do things. Westerners must respect Muslim ways of thinking and behaving and allow Muslims to devise solutions to their problems that conform to the religious beliefs of their people.

Muslims and Westerners live closer together today than at any time in the past. This has created a need for greater understanding, but it is also an opportunity for cultural growth. Throughout the past 1,500 years of history, both Islamic and Western cultures have enriched human civilization. With effort and understanding, Western and Islamic cultures can enrich each other in the future.

Text-Dependent Questions

1. What is Hezbollah?
2. How have Western nations attempted to prevent the spread of the Islamic State of Iraq and the Levant?

 Research Project

In late 2010, sparked by the self-immolation of a fruit vendor in Tunisia, anti-government protests began to erupt throughout the Arab world. The ongoing protests are aimed at improving the political circumstances and living conditions of the Arab people, and have become known in the West as the "Arab Spring." Using your school library or the internet, find out more about the origin of the Arab Spring protests. Take a blank map of the Arab countries (one can be printed online from http://commons.wikimedia.org/wiki/File:Arab_world_location_map.svg). Label and mark the countries where protesters succeeded in overthrowing or changing governments.

Series Glossary

BCE and CE—alternatives to the traditional Western designation of calendar eras, which used the birth of Jesus as a dividing line. BCE stands for "Before the Common Era," and is equivalent to BC ("Before Christ"). Dates labeled CE, or "Common Era," are equivalent to Anno Domini (AD, or "the Year of Our Lord").

Hadith—the body of customs, sayings, and traditions ascribed to the prophet Muhammad and his closest companions in the early Muslim community, as recorded by those who witnessed them.

hajj—the fifth pillar of Islam; a pilgrimage to Mecca, which all Muslims who are able are supposed to make at least once in their lifetime.

imam—a Muslim spiritual leader. In the Sunni tradition, an imam is a religious leader who leads the community in prayer. In the Shiite tradition, an imam is a descendant of Muhammad who is the divinely chosen and infallible leader of the community.

jihad—struggle. To Muslims, the "greater jihad" refers to an individual's struggle to live a pure life, while the "lesser jihad" refers to defensive struggle or warfare against oppression and the enemies of Islam.

Qur'an—Islam's holy scriptures, which contain Allah's revelations to the prophet Muhammad in the early seventh century.

Sharia—a traditional system of Islamic law based on the Qur'an, the opinion of Islamic leaders, and the desires of the community.

Shia—one of the two major sects of Islam; members of this sect are called Shiites.

Sufism—a mystical tradition that emphasizes the inner aspect of spirituality through meditation and remembrance of God.

Sunna—the traditions of the prophet Muhammad as exemplified by his actions and words, and preserved in the Qur'an and Hadith.

Sunni—the largest sect of Islam; the name is derived from the Arabic phrase "the Path," referring to those who follow the instructions of Muhammad as recorded in the Qur'an and other ancient writings or traditions.

umma—the worldwide community of Muslims.

Further Reading

Cesari, Jocelyne. *Why the West Fears Islam: An Exploration of Muslims in Liberal Democracies*. New York: Palgrave Macmillan, 2013.

Curiel, Jonathan. *Islam in America*. London: I.B. Tauris, 2015.

Green, Todd H. *The Fear of Islam: An Introduction to Islamophobia in the West*. Minneapolis: Fortress Press, 2015.

Harris, Sam, and Maajid Nawaz. *Islam and the Future of Tolerance: A Dialogue*. Cambridge, Mass.: Harvard University Press, 2015.

Hazleton, Lesley. *After the Prophet: The Epic Story of the Shia-Sunni Split in Islam*. New York: Doubleday, 2010.

Madden, Thomas F. *The Concise History of the Crusades*. Lanham, Md.: Rowman & Littlefield, 2013.

Mandaville, Peter. *Islam and Politics*. 2nd ed. New York: Routledge, 2014.

Mansfield, Peter. *A History of the Middle East*. 4th ed. revised and updated by Nicholas Pelham. New York: Penguin Books, 2013.

Ramadan, Tariq. *Islam, the West, and the Challenges of Modernity*. Leicester, UK: The Islamic Foundation, 2009.

Internet Resources

http://islam.com

A portal with information about Islam, including discussion forums, articles, and links to other resources.

http://www.fordham.edu/halsall/islam/islamsbook.html

Fordham University provides this online Islamic History Sourcebook, with links to texts from every period in the history of Islam, as well as maps and other resources.

http://www.cair.com/

The Council on American-Islamic Relations (CAIR) is an organization dedicated to providing an Islamic perspective on issues of importance to the American people.

http://www.merip.org/primer-palestine-israel-arab-israeli-conflict-new

This site provides an overview of the Israeli-Arab conflict over Palestine.

http://www.homelandsecurity.com

This is the official site of the Terrorism Research Center, a private organization that studies terrorism. It includes articles about terrorism and the United States.

http://www.pbs.org/wgbh/pages/frontline/shows/muslims/themes/west.html

The PBS program *Frontline* hosts this page, which includes interview excerpts from prominent Muslim scholars and leaders about the conflict between Islam and the West.

Index

Numbers in **bold italic** refer to captions.

Index

Index

Index

Index

Picture Credits

Contributors

Senior Consultant CAMILLE PECASTAING, PH.D., is acting director of the Middle East Studies Program at the Paul H. Nitze School of Advanced International Studies at Johns Hopkins University. A student of behavioral sciences and historical sociology, Dr. Pecastaing's research focuses on the cognitive and emotive foundations of xenophobic political cultures and ethnoreligious violence, using the Muslim world and its European and Asian peripheries as a case study. He has written on political Islam, Islamist terrorism, social change, and globalization. Pecastaing's essays have appeared in many journals, including World Affairs and Policy Review. He is the author of *Jihad in the Arabian Sea* (Hoover Institution Press, 2011).

General Editor DR. SHAMS INATI is a Professor of Islamic Studies at Villanova University. She is a specialist in Islamic philosophy and theology and has published widely in the field. Her publications include *Remarks and Admonitions, Part One: Logic* (1984), *Our Philosophy* (1987), *Ibn Sina and Mysticism* (1996), *The Second Republic of Lebanon* (1999), *The Problem of Evil: Ibn Sina's Theodicy* (2000), and *Iraq: Its History, People, and Politics* (2003). She has also written a large number of articles that have appeared in books, journals, and encyclopedias.

Dr. Inati has been the recipient of a number of awards and honors, including an Andrew Mellon Fellowship, an Endowment for the Humanities grant, a US Department of Defense grant, and a Fulbright grant. For further information about her work, see www.homepage.villanova.edu/shams.inati.

TAYYIB OMAR has lived in the eastern, southern and midwestern United States, and in central and western Canada. He has written on cultural studies and issues in contemporary philosophy. He and his family currently live on the outskirts of Washington D.C.